DOM HELDER
CAMARA

DOM HELDER CAMARA

Essential Writings

Selected with an Introduction by

FRANCIS MCDONAGH

ORBIS BOOKS

Maryknoll, New York 10545

Founded in 1970, Orbis Books endeavors to publish works that enlighten the mind, nourish the spirit, and challenge the conscience. The publishing arm of the Mary-knoll Fathers and Brothers, Orbis seeks to explore the global dimensions of the Christian faith and mission, to invite dialogue with diverse cultures and religious traditions, and to serve the cause of reconciliation and peace. The books published reflect the views of their authors and do not represent the official position of the Maryknoll Society. To learn more about Maryknoll and Orbis Books, please visit our website at www.maryknoll.org.

Selections from *Sister Earth* used with permission of New City Press. Selections from *Charismatic Renewal and Social Action* used with permission of Darton, Longman, & Todd.

Queries regarding rights and permissions should be addressed to:
Orbis Books, P.O. Box 308, Maryknoll, NY 10545-0308.

Manufactured in the United States of America.

Library of Congress Cataloging-in-Publication Data

Câmara, Hélder, 1909–1999.
　　[Selections. English. 2009]
　　Dom Hélder Câmara : essential writings / selected with an introduction by Francis McDonagh.
　　　　p.　cm. – (Modern spiritual masters series)
　　ISBN 978-1-57075-823-2 (pbk.)
　　　　1. Theology. 2. Catholic Church – Doctrines. 3. Christian sociology – Catholic Church. I. McDonagh, Francis. II. Title.
　　BX4705.C2625A25 2009
　　230′.2 – dc22

2008050454

Contents

Sources

CB   Dom Helder Camara, *The Conversions of a Bishop: An Interview with José de Broucker* (London: Collins, 1979).

CC   *The Church and Colonialism* (New York: Dimension, 1969; London: Sheed and Ward, 1969).

CRSA   *Charismatic Renewal and Social Action: A Dialogue,* Helder Camara and Léon-Joseph Suenens (London: Darton, Longman & Todd, 1980).

DF   *The Desert Is Fertile* (Maryknoll, N.Y.: Orbis Books, 1974).

ML   *It's Midnight, Lord* (Washington, D.C.: Pastoral Press, 1974).

SE   *Sister Earth* (Hyde Park, N.Y.: New City Press, 1990).

TTG   *Through the Gospel with Dom Helder Camara* (Maryknoll, N.Y.: Orbis Books, 1986).

VP   *Dom Helder Camara: The Violence of a Peacemaker* by José de Broucker (Maryknoll, N.Y.: Orbis Books, 1970).

Acknowledgments

Anyone writing about Dom Helder outside Brazil owes an immense debt to José de Broucker. His two book-length interviews with Dom Helder during the 1970s, published in translation as *The Violence of a Peacemaker* (1970) and *Conversions of a Bishop* (1979) give a real insight into his personality and the background to his work, especially in his early days as archbishop of Olinda and Recife.

In Brazil I would like to thank Zildo Rocha and Luiz Carlos Marques for their time and insights, and Oscar Beozzo for sharing unpublished work on Dom Helder. I owe a debt to my editor, Robert Ellsberg, for his patience and advice. I also wish to thank Dinah and Grace Livingstone for their support and encouragement.

Introduction

Dom Helder in Context

The Importance of Dom Helder

Helder Camara, like the Second Vatican Council, is probably a distant historical reference to most Catholics under fifty. The Brazilian archbishop was a key actor in the Council, which forty years later, is still a reference for Catholics, though in recent years subject to different interpretations. Many see that meeting of the world's Catholic bishops as irrevocably changing the direction of the Roman Catholic Church, or at least forcing it to regard issues of global justice, war, and peace as integral to its mission rather than a secondary topic in a dusty volume of "Catholic Social Teaching." Socially aware Catholics may be aware of Camara's famous phrase: "When I give food to the poor, they call me a saint. When I ask why the poor have no food, they call me a communist."

The importance of Dom Helder, as he is most often known following the Brazilian style of address, is that he did not reduce Christianity to a political or social movement; he believed, in the words of Jesus in Matthew's Gospel, that "just as you did it to one of the least of these who are members of my family, you did it to me" (Matt. 25:40). Dom Helder talked about the "real presence" of Christ, not just in the bread and wine of the Eucharist, but in the poor. This was part of his first message to his diocese:

> Although for some people it may appear strange, I declare that here in the North-East Christ is called José, Antônio, Severino. *Ecce Homo!* Here is Christ the Human! The

11

human being who needs justice, has the right to justice, deserves justice.[1]

For Dom Helder, the reforms introduced by the Second Vatican Council have as their ultimate goal to transform the church into "a church of service and poverty," one that would promote "the dialog of the two worlds," the rich and the poor. Themes such as globalization and climate change, which seem to be characteristic of our twenty-first century, are also present in Dom Helder's writing, albeit in different terminology. No wonder that a theologian who worked with him, José Comblin, called him: "a bishop for the twenty-first century."

Dom Helder held firmly to his Christian and Catholic faith, but believed equally firmly that God inspired people of goodwill from other faith traditions or none. He placed his hope for a better world in minorities within all institutions. He called these "Abrahamic minorities," while apologizing for the fact that the term would seem alien to those outside the traditions of Judaism, Christianity, or Islam: for him these minorities included adherents of other faiths as well as atheists. "Macro-ecumenism" is the term applied to this attitude today.

The least known aspect of Dom Helder is his "meditations," the texts he wrote daily during his vigils between two and five in the morning, to "achieve an inner unity." This was a man who claimed to be "always seeing the unclouded Christ." His delight in nature, wind, water and fire, plants and animals, points us toward what we regard as a modern concern with the "unity of creation." Reading these writings is to be drawn into a familiar world that suddenly reveals unexpected aspects. There is a mixture of naiveté and depth, but a tone that avoids pretentiousness through a constant vein of irony and self-mockery. One of his best interpreters to the outside world, the French journalist José de Broucker, captured this strangeness:

> It is always disturbing to meet a man possessed by a faith like this; a man who not only believes in a living, present

1. Inaugural sermon, quoted in Mary Hall, *The Impossible Dream: The Spirituality of Dom Helder Camara* (Maryknoll, N.Y.: Orbis Books, 1980), 75.

God, but actually enacts his beliefs. The history that he relates and makes is illuminated with a strange transparency. Can things really be so simple? You feel you may be succumbing to the charms of poetry, to visions of Utopia. You have to summon all the arguments of critical reason to stop yourself tumbling into what looks like the naiveté of childhood.

It is impossible to avoid this kind of confusion with Dom Helder. Listening to or reading his words is like listening to or reading the holy scriptures: the story of a creation and a liberation which God has asked man to complete. Listening to or reading his words, you run the risk of seeing our world, today's world and tomorrow's world, through the eyes of the God of believers. It is a severe test of both reason and faith.[2]

Another explanation of this paradox is that Dom Helder was, in the words of Richard Shaull, "a man of faith whose eyes are fixed on the future rather than the past."

A Brief Biography

Helder Pessoa Camara was born on February 7, 1909, in Fortaleza, capital of the north-eastern Brazilian state of Ceará. His father, João, was an accountant in the main private company of the state, and his mother, Adelaide, was a primary school teacher. Helder's parents were not rich, needing Adelaide's earnings to supplement João's salary and also receiving a rent support payment from the state, but they were well connected to the state's conservative political elite, so much so that one of the witnesses at their marriage was the state governor. João was a Freemason, but at the same time a practicing Catholic, and the family home included a tiny chapel, where, in the month of May, he led the family in evening devotions to Our

---

2. Dom Helder Camara, *The Conversions of a Bishop: An Interview with José de Broucker* (London: Collins, 1979), 12.

Lady, including the whole rosary recited in Latin. Of the thirteen children born to the couple, six died in childhood, four
from an epidemic of croup in 1905, one from meningitis in
1906, and the sixth from gangrene after being knocked over by
a bicycle in 1909. Even a middle-class family in Fortaleza in this
period was at the mercy of the precarious state of health care:
the vaccines against croup had to come from Rio de Janeiro by
boat and arrived too late to save the Camara children. This family tragedy is the origin of Helder's unusual name. João insisted
that the traditional family names had brought bad luck and
opened an atlas that Adelaide used for preparing her lessons;
his eye was caught by the name Den Helder on a promontory
in northern Holland.[3]

Helder's mother gave her lessons in the family home, and
her own children were naturally among her pupils. The son re-
members her as tender underneath her strictness, and also as
rejecting the prudishness of contemporary culture:

> I can still see her now, in the big classroom. I have so many
> memories of her. Whenever I think of injustice, I remem-
> ber my mother. She felt that her own children should set
> an example to the rest: so she was very strict with us. One
> day when I was little she set me a task that was really too
> difficult for me. I couldn't solve the problem and burst into
> tears. My mother stood up abruptly, and I thought she was
> going to cane me — even though she never had before. But
> instead she handed me a little picture with an inscription:
> "To my son, of whom I ask too much."
>
> My mother helped me enormously. She taught me a
> great deal. I remember one day when we were talking she
> pointed to her face (she often spoke with her hands) and
> said to me: "When you are older, many people will tell
> you that this was created by God, this" — pointing to her

3. Nelson Piletti and Walter Práxedes, *Dom Helder Camara: Entre o poder e a profecia* (São Paulo: Atica, 1997), 28. Unless otherwise indicated, details described here come from this work.

bosom — "by who knows what, and the rest" — indicating the rest of her body — "by the devil. But it isn't true, my son! From your head to your toes, you are God's creature!" I was five years old at the time, but her words made a great impression on me. And I think that incident will give you an idea of how unconventional her views were at a time when it was normal to look for sin everywhere.[4]

From an early age, Helder played at saying Mass, and he describes the following conversation with his father, when he was eight or nine:

> "Son, you're growing up and you keep on saying you want to be a priest, but do you really know what it means to be a priest. Did you know that to be a priest you can't be selfish, you can't just think about yourself? Being a priest and being selfish is impossible; they're two things that don't go together. Priests believe that when they celebrate the Eucharist, Christ himself becomes present. Have you ever thought what hands that directly touch Christ should be like?"
>
> When the boy replied, "Dad, I want to be a priest like that," João said, "Then God bless you. God bless you. You know we don't have much money, but I'll figure out how to help you get into the seminary."

One snapshot of Helder as a boy that seems to prefigure his zeal and talent for communicating his message is that he would make up stories and tell them to younger children, and the occasional adult, in the yard of the family house.

There was a literary tradition in the family. Helder's paternal grandfather had been a newspaper editor, and his father was a theater critic for the local papers. Helder recalls him reading plays to the family and singing songs from classical operas, and he would take his children to the theater. The familiarity with the French language and culture that later helped Helder's international work began here. The port city of Fortaleza had

---

4. Camara, *The Conversions of a Bishop*, 29–30.

connections with France, and João was given French news-
papers and magazines by his French boss. His brother, Gilberto,
twelve years older, was already beginning a career as a critic
and dramatist; he was a subscriber to the literary review produced by the French newspaper *Le Figaro* and received regular
deliveries of books from France. Gilberto introduced Helder to
French literature.

Helder's knowledge of French and French culture was con-
solidated in the local seminary, staffed by French and Dutch
Lazarist priests. Helder attracted attention for his seriousness
and got good grades, though he was not at the top of his
class. One trait that marked him out was his awkward questions. On one famous occasion he challenged the rector, who
had opened Helder's locked desk and taken some poems the
young seminarian had written. When some weeks later Helder
had said nothing, the rector summoned him. Helder's argument
was: "Father Rector, I knew that you would feel bad having
to admit that you'd gone to the classroom with a flashlight at
night like a thief and taken my papers." When the rector apologized and offered to give him the second desk key that he kept,
Helder insisted that all the students should have both keys to
their desks, and the rector agreed. The origin of the problem
was that the rector was worried that Helder was writing poetry,
or meditations in verse form: "Poetry can carry us away, further
than we want." Helder agreed to stop writing his poems until
his ordination.

Helder read widely, and another challenge to his seminary
rector came when the rector offered him a book with some
pages stapled together on the grounds that the passages were
not suitable for a seminarian. Helder refused the book, arguing
that if he wasn't trusted to avoid unsuitable passages, he didn't
want the book. In the end he helped to advise the staff on books
that the students ought to read.

Helder's interest in social issues was already keen before his
ordination, and this was channeled into the conservative version
of social Catholicism promoted by the leader of the Brazilian
church, Cardinal Sebastião Leme. He sought to challenge the

reduction of the church's influence following the creation of a republic and the separation of church and state under the constitution of 1891. For Helder, this developed into a passionate involvement in the Brazilian "Integralist" movement, an authoritarian, nationalist movement influenced by European fascism that for many Catholics seemed the logical implication of the church's teaching in the social domain. So caught up was Helder in these ideas that for some months at the end of his theology course he seriously considered giving up the priesthood to dedicate himself to politics. Having finally decided to continue his vocation, he was ordained on August 15, 1931, at the early age of twenty-two, two years below the age fixed in canon law.

After ordination, asked by his bishop to supervise the Catholic workers movement in Ceará and appointed chaplain to the Catholic teachers' league, Father Helder began to bring these groups into the orbit of the Integralist organization, the Ceará Labor League. He eventually became one of the leaders of the Integralist movement in the state. Catholics organized to press for the teaching of religion in public schools, but this led them also to attack the important movement to introduce modern educational techniques. In 1934 Helder led a walkout at a conference in Fortaleza addressed by leading educators before, a few days later, leading a band of thugs that assaulted the educators, the green shirt of the Integralist movement visible under his cassock. He became a leading figure in the Catholic education campaign, traveling to various states, and gaining a national reputation.

In 1930 Getúlio Vargas seized power in Brazil, initiating fifteen years of authoritarian rule. He received the support of Cardinal Leme, and in return the constitution of 1934 allowed religious education in public schools. In Helder's Ceará, however, the church supported candidates opposed to the Vargas government, and the archbishop of Fortaleza summoned Father Helder back from Rio to Ceará to tour the state ordering Catholics to vote for the candidates of the Catholic Electoral League in the elections of 1934. In return for this support, the new governor offered Helder the post of education secretary in the state, which, on an order from his archbishop, he reluctantly accepted. It should be noted that, faced with the dire state of education in Ceará, he sought help from the very educators he had denounced so recently.

This was not a happy time for the young priest. In August 1935, his mother died. His energy in his ministerial post provoked the envy of other ministers, and his continued involvement in the Integralist movement became an embarrassment to the archbishop. Helder's solution was to use his contacts in Rio to obtain a post in the education ministry in the capital, and he moved to Rio in 1936. This was to be the beginning of a new stage in his ideological development, as well as consolidating his reputation as a national figure and eventually launching him onto the international scene.

In Rio, Father Helder was warmly welcomed by Cardinal Leme, and he continued the work he had begun in Ceará as an administrator in public education. In 1939 he passed a public examination to become a recognized expert, thus becoming a civil servant. This role was not merely technical, but also highly political. President Vargas had given the church informal control over Brazilian education in return for its support in 1930, and Helder became a member of an elite group that promoted the church's interests in the world of education. So important was his role that Cardinal Leme refused his request to resign and dedicate himself entirely to preaching. This was the other activity into which the thirty-year-old priest threw himself on his arrival in Rio, and he acquired a reputation as a preacher and retreat-giver with a wide sense of culture and a passionate delivery. From 1941 he also lectured in various Catholic colleges, including what later became the Pontifical University of Rio de Janeiro. The cultural life of the capital brought Helder into contact with the cream of Brazilian intelligentsia, including, for example, the young novelist Jorge Amado.

The passion to communicate that had led Helder as a boy to make up stories to entertain children in Fortaleza was still strong in the priest and preacher. In 1938 he wrote that he wanted "to speak the thousand modern dialects, to talk like the people of today" to communicate "the immortal, eternal message, the divine Word." This passion led him also to propose a reform of the teaching of religion, ironically adopting the modern techniques that he had previously opposed as "materialism" in his battles to defend Catholic education. The faith, he insisted, was not a subject that "can only be presented in rigid, mummified formulas that can only be taught in a boring and unpleasant way."

Cardinal Leme died in 1942 and was succeeded by Cardinal Jaime de Barros Camara, no relation to Helder, though tracing their ancestry back to three eighteenth-century immigrants from Madeira became a joke between them. Helder established warm relations with his new archbishop, who appreciated his talents, to the point of requesting that he be appointed auxiliary bishop. Father Helder continued in government service until 1946, when he was allowed to resign and devote himself to his priestly ministry. His first task was to organize a national conference for Catholic Action, the movement launched by Pope Pius XI in 1927 in which lay people would be trained to promote Catholic values in a rapidly changing society. This led to an appointment as national director of the organization. Previously Catholic Action had been organized at a purely national level, in the way that Father Helder had organized workers in Fortaleza in the early 1930s, but now Helder traveled round Brazil discussing the need for a new model of Catholic Action.

Brazil was rapidly industrializing, and emigration from the rural areas had created poor communities around the great cities. Unions were forming, and the Communist Party had won around 10 percent of the vote in the 1945 elections. In Rio Helder's friend Father José Távora had founded the Young Christian Workers (JOC in Portuguese) to promote Catholic values among the growing working class, and Helder immediately incorporated JOC into the structure of Catholic Action throughout Brazil. This work gave Helder a broader understanding of the social conditions in Brazil, as well as bringing him into contact with the most influential members of the Brazilian hierarchy. At the suggestion of one bishop, Helder proposed the creation of a national secretariat, and the idea was accepted in 1947, with Helder appointed to head the office. Having been given responsibility but no funds, Helder once again demonstrated his talent for using his contacts, this time among the middle-class young people who had been part of his Catholic Action group in Rio, and soon had an office and staff.

The new secretariat was highly significant. For the first time, the Brazilian Catholic Church had a national structure dedicated to social issues, with an embryonic form of what later became known as "the preferential option for the poor." Catholic Action was a model for Helder's subsequent proposal for a national bishops conference.

These years in Rio were important for Helder personally. Through one of his students, Virgínia Cortes de Lacerda, he got to know a group of young middle-class women involved in Catholic Action. The group would meet on Friday evenings to listen to music and talk. Conversation ranged beyond the concerns of Catholic Action to the rich cultural life of Rio, including literature, poetry, and the theater. Father Helder helped these conservative young women appreciate works at odds with their Catholic tradition, such as the plays of Nelson Rodrigues. This group of friends became Helder's base and support system for the rest of his life, and he called them, significantly, his "family"; he wrote to them when traveling and they in return helped to provide material for his talks. From 1938 various members of Helder's birth family also moved to Rio, including finally his father, João, on his retirement in 1942, sharing a small house in the neighborhood of Botafogo. Space was at a premium, and Helder shared a bedroom with his father.

During his time in Rio Helder gradually moved away from fascism, but it was not an easy process. When he arrived in Rio, Cardinal Leme ordered him to sever his links with the Brazilian Integralist movement, but personal ties and friendships were harder to break. And, when it looked as though the Integralists might come to power with Getúlio Vargas's 1937 coup, Leme allowed Helder to accept an invitation to join the movement's Higher Council. But when Vargas banned political parties, the Integralists attempted a rising and were crushed. Since there was no longer any benefit to the church from an association with the movement, the cardinal reinstated his prohibition of any involvement by Helder in the movement, or in any political party.

Helder's views were also changing, in part due to the influence of the French thinker Jacques Maritain, whose book *True Humanism* was being discussed in Brazil beginning in 1936. Maritain argued for Catholic acceptance of democracy and a pluralistic society — in the 1930s a radical break with the view that the Catholic notion of "order" meant authoritarian government to defend private property and an idealized family. Nonetheless, as late as 1946, Cardinal Jaime de Barros Camara's request to have Father Helder made auxiliary bishop of Rio was rejected on the grounds that he was identified with the Integralist movement.[5]

But Helder was not out of favor in Vatican circles. In 1948 the nuncio, Carlo Chiarlo, invited him to be a counselor to the nunciature, an unofficial post, but an honor, and one that entailed weekly visits on Saturday mornings to review the situation of Brazilian church and society. This was a position of enormous influence, since the nuncio managed the process by which bishops were appointed, as well as the relations between the Vatican and the Brazilian government. Helder was to retain the position for sixteen years and developed an even closer friendship with the next nuncio, Armando Lombardi, who firmly supported the appointment of socially committed bishops in the country until his sudden death in 1964.

The year 1950 was decreed a Holy Year, and Helder, now with the honorific title of Monsignor, was entrusted with the task of organizing the Brazilian celebrations. One of the more bizarre of these was a pilgrimage to Rome on an overcrowded troop ship that the Brazilian government was persuaded to donate, whose thirteen hundred passengers notably included

5. Marcos de Castro, *Dom Helder: Misticismo e santidade* (Rio de Janeiro: Civilização Brasileira, 2002), 74.

four prostitutes — who promised Monsignor Helder that they wouldn't cause scandal during the pilgrimage, and that their goal was to advance their careers in Paris. It was thus, as part chaplain, part tour guide, that Helder Camara first set foot in the center of world Catholicism. Helder was not part of the group of Brazilian pilgrims received in audience by Pope Pius XII, but he was invited back in December 1950 for the evaluation of the Holy Year. On this occasion the nuncio secured him an appointment with the Vatican sub-secretary of state, Monsignor Giovanni Batista Montini, in order to propose the creation of a Brazilian bishops conference, an idea he had been discussing with senior Brazilian bishops. Montini and Helder immediately got along, and this friendship was to become even more significant when Montini became Pope Paul VI.

The first meeting of the Brazilian bishops conference was held on October 14, 1952, and Helder, finally made a bishop in March of that year, was elected secretary general by acclamation. He held the post for twelve years. Brazil thus became the fourth country, after France, the United States, and Canada, to have a national church administration. Given the church's influence in Brazilian society, and its political power, this body was to be of enormous significance as Brazil headed for a period of social convulsion, culminating in the military dictatorship of 1964–85.

The trends represented by Dom Helder were also operating in other Latin American countries. The bishop of Talca in Chile, Manuel Larraín, had been working for the creation of a continental body of bishops for Latin America. This was finally approved by the Vatican in 1954, and Dom Helder's friend Monsignor Montini suggested to him that the International Eucharistic Congress planned for 1955, which Dom Helder was responsible for organizing, might be a suitable opportunity for an assembly of Latin American bishops. This duly took place between July 25 and August 4, 1955, resulting in the creation of the Latin American Episcopal Council, or CELAM in its Spanish acronym. This process brought together

Camara and Larraín, who became close friends and allies in CELAM and, significantly, at the Second Vatican Council ten years later.

Dom Helder maintained a schedule that would have killed most people. It took three teams of assistants to keep up with him, according to one of his helpers. His day began, as it had since his days as a seminarian, at 2:00 a.m., when he was awakened by his alarm and spent three hours in prayer, meditation, dealing with correspondence, and preparing talks. He would then sleep for an hour from 5:00 to 6:00, when he would rise to begin his public activities. It was in this period of quiet before dawn that he wrote the "poems" that his seminary rector had worried about. (At the time of his death they totaled seven thousand, only a small number of which have been published to date.)

In Rio a typical day would mean Mass at 6:00, after which he would be besieged by people seeking help. He would then go to the archbishop's palace to deal with his duties as auxiliary bishop and secretary general of the bishops conference. Lunch would be in a simple restaurant near the archbishop's palace, where "steak Dom Helder" was later added to the menu in his honor — not that he ever ate the whole steak, which he usually shared with an assistant. The afternoon was devoted to meetings with bishops. In the evenings, Dom Helder would give talks or, increasingly, appear on TV shows.

Dom Helder was, in short, a celebrity, in demand to officiate at baptisms and weddings. According to his biographers, it became a status symbol in Rio to have one's children baptized or married by him. The media mogul Roberto Marinho asked him to be godfather to his son, which gave Dom Helder access to what was then one of the most influential media, Radio Globo, where for several years he had a daily program entitled *Our Daily Bread*. In the political world as well, Dom Helder had easy access to successive presidents, Vargas, Goulart, Kubitschek. But he also enjoyed music, theater, and cinema. Saturday nights were for visiting friends and listening to music in cafés or going to a show. At birthday parties, he was an eager participant in the games and songs.[6]

The 1950s and 1960s were to see further developments in Dom Helder's understanding of poverty. One element of this he attributed to a conversation with the French cardinal Gerlier, one of the many prelates from around the world who attended the 1955 International Eucharistic Congress in Rio. Helder later described the encounter to the French journalist José de Broucker as follows:

> Among all the cardinals who attended was old Cardinal Gerlier of Lyons. He insisted on speaking to me before returning to France. I was very busy by now, organizing the assembly of Latin American bishops, so he had difficulty in tracking me down. But since he was a cardinal, and a Frenchman, and a friend, we managed to arrange a meeting. Cardinal Gerlier said to me: "I was determined to see you because there's something I must say to you before I leave. I have had some experience in organization, and it's clear to me that the reason this congress has gone so well is because there was a talented organizer in charge. And that's the reason why I insisted on seeing you. May I speak to you as a brother, a brother in baptism, a brother in the priesthood, a brother in the episcopate, a brother in Christ? Brother Dom Helder, why don't you use this organizing talent that the Lord has given you in the service of the poor? You must know that although Rio de Janeiro is one of the most beautiful cities in the world, it is also one of the most hideous, because all these *favelas* in such a beautiful setting are an insult to the Lord."
>
> And so the grace of the Lord came to me through the presence of Cardinal Gerlier. Not just through the words he spoke: behind his words was the presence of a whole life, a whole conviction. And I was moved by the grace of the Lord. I was thrown to the ground like Saul on the road to Damascus.

6. Piletti and Práxedes, *Dom Helder Camara*, 217–19.

I kissed the cardinal's hands: "This is a turning point in my life! I will dedicate myself to the poor! I'm not so sure that I have a particular talent for organization, but I will offer all the Lord has given me in the service of the poor."[7]

After the Eucharistic Congress, Dom Helder threw himself, with typical energy, into various anti-poverty programs, a low-cost housing program and a soft loans program, the Providence Bank. But these were mere band-aids that did nothing to deal with deeper causes of the immigration flooding into Rio from desperately poor rural communities all over Brazil. He later described the inadequacy of these programs, with typical self-mockery, in the same interview with José de Broucker:

Our plans sounded wonderful; but unfortunately they became embroiled in petty party politics. There was about to be an election. Every time we took a family out of the *favela* some politician would come along and put two or three or four families in its place. "Wait there and Dom Helder will build you a new flat!" It was terrible. People could see that the St. Sebastian Crusade didn't take long to build its flats; and they were all prepared to come and wait their turn in the slums. By the time our first project was completed we realized that instead of being wiped out the population of the *favela* had doubled.... But our work did have one effect that we hadn't expected: the city of Rio de Janeiro finally opened its eyes to the *favelas,* and the authorities began to be concerned about them. We had forced them to take notice. Until then the problem didn't exist, because officially the *favelas* didn't exist. The *favelas* were never mentioned in urban development programs: Why bring in water and electricity? Why build sewers, since the *favelas* didn't exist?

The real problem, Dom Helder later came to see, had to do with the way Brazil was industrializing:

---

7. Camara, *The Conversions of a Bishop,* 151–52.

I understand it even better now that I am here in the
North-East. Every day the agriculture industry expels more
peasants from the interior. The big companies move in with
their modern methods of cultivation which require far fewer
hands and produce much higher yields. They buy vast tracts
of land, and anyone who has been living there — probably without any official documents but often for several
generations — is forced to leave. They're simply thrown out.

And they go to the towns. If they can, they go to Rio
de Janeiro or São Paulo. São Paulo has nearly 8 million
inhabitants. It's the largest city in the North-East: in other
words there are more North-Easterners in São Paulo than
in any other city in the North-East. The peasants think
that they'll be able to find houses, schools, work, and
hospitals in the city. And they end up in the *favelas*.

The other event that brought the various strands of Dom
Helder's thinking and experience together was the Second Vatican Council. This totally unexpected initiative on the part of
Pope John XXIII to open the church up the modern world, not
to adapt to it in a passive sense, but to understand it, dialog
with it, and then to evangelize it, released energies that had been
paralyzed by the church's battle with science and the liberal
and democratic revolutions. The dominant ideas that shaped
the Council had been forming in Europe and North America.
Dom Helder and his fellow bishops from the global South ab-
sorbed these ideas, but then tried to draw the attention of the
Council, and so of the worldwide church, to the imbalance in
the global system, the gulf between rich and poor.

The story of the theological battle at the start of the Council
between the world's bishops and the conservative Vatican bu-
reaucracy has often been told. The other story, of the attempt
to move the church closer to the poor in its style of life and
its social and political options, is less well known, and it is this
story that has Dom Helder as one of its heroes.

Pope John XXIII announced his surprise decision to convene
an ecumenical council on January 25, 1959, but the Council did

not meet until October 1962. The intervening years were a period of preparation, and Dom Helder was one of ten Brazilian bishops appointed to preparatory commissions. But Helder was also a friend of Cardinal Montini (a key adviser to the pope, and later to become pope himself during the Council), secretary of the third largest bishops conference in the world (after those of the United States and Italy), and vice-president of the only continental organization of bishops, the Latin American Episcopal Council, or CELAM. The other vice-president of CELAM was his friend and fellow reformer, Manuel Larraín. The two men set out to mobilize key figures in support of the reform agenda. Dom Helder's fluent French enabled him to establish a relationship with Cardinal Suenens, archbishop of Brussels, who became a friend, and with the secretary of the French bishops conference, the future cardinal Roger Etchegaray.

The residence of the Brazilian bishops during the Council was known as Domus Mariae, and this became the base for a range of meetings and lectures to promote various aspects of church renewal and especially a dialog between the church in the rich world and the church in the poor world, the "dialog of the two worlds," as he called it. Dom Helder organized regular Friday lectures by theologians on topics relevant to the Council's agenda, ninety in all by the end of the Council, and these became obligatory for observers who wanted to understand the new directions. Among the Friday lecturers were Hans Küng and Dominican Yves Congar. Congar was impressed by Dom Helder, whom he described as "not only very open, but full of ideas, imagination and enthusiasm. He has what is missing in Rome — 'vision.' "[8]

Another important figure whom Dom Helder brought in as an adviser was the French priest Louis Lebret, an expert on development issues, who advised the bishops on the document "The Church in the Modern World" and was later influential in the drafting of Paul VI's encyclical *Populorum Progressio.*

---

8. Y.-M. Congar, *Mon Journal du Concile,* 87, quoted by J. O. Beozzo, "Dom Helder Camara e o Concílio Vaticano II," in Zildo Rocha, ed., *Helder, o Dom,* 3rd ed. (Petrópolis: Vozes, 2000), 108.

Nothing if not ambitious, Dom Helder tried to unite the bishops of Africa and Asia into organizations on the CELAM model and even a conference representing all the bishops of the Third World, an "inter-conference." The cause underlying all the others, however, was to transform the church into "a church of service and poverty," after the title of a famous tract by Congar. By the end of the Council he had gathered a group of eighty-six bishops, who became known as "the church of the poor," and, in a ceremony in the Roman catacombs, solemnly pledged themselves to lives of evangelical simplicity and dedicated themselves to the cause of the poor. As it became clear that world poverty would not become a major theme for the Council, Dom Helder pressed his old friend Montini, by now Pope Paul VI, to issue an encyclical on the subject, which duly appeared in 1967 as *Populorum Progressio*, "On the Development of Peoples."

The other direction in which Dom Helder took his concern with poverty was CELAM, creating a tradition in which the Latin American bishops produced their own distinctive body of teaching, focusing on the need for a church commitment to justice and giving the church's backing to the "preferential option for the poor." These ideas were propagated in a series of "General Conferences" of the Latin American bishops. The first and most radical of these was held in Medellín, Colombia, in 1968, which sought to translate the vision of Vatican II into Latin American terms. In subsequent conferences, especially in the Mexican city of Puebla (1979), there were fierce battles as conservatives, generally supported by Pope John Paul II, tried to correct the "Marxist" exaggerations of Medellín. Nevertheless, in the latest CELAM conference, in Aparecida, Brazil, in May 2007, attended by Pope Benedict XVI, there was surprising consensus on the need for the church to update its message of liberation to address poverty and its causes in a world of HIV and AIDS and globalization. Latin America remains the only continent where the bishops have developed a distinctive body of teaching and a tradition of formulating their position, both to the faithful and to the world at large, and Dom Helder's contribution to this is undoubtedly one of his most important achievements.

According to a leading historian of the church in Brazil, Dom Helder's work at the Council "transformed him from the relatively little known auxiliary archbishop of Rio de Janeiro into one of the most influential personalities on the contemporary international church scene,"[9] but his international reputation was also enhanced by the lectures he gave outside Brazil after being silenced by the military regime.

In Brazil in the 1950s social tensions were building up. Industrialization in rural areas was intensifying the exodus to the cities, where the lack of housing and infrastructure made conditions little better than on the land. Unions and social organizations, including the radical Young Christian Students, were pressing for "basic reforms." Military leaders tried to prevent the radical João Goulart from taking over as president in 1961, but were foiled. At the same time, Dom Helder's more radical position was beginning to cause difficulties in his relationship with the politically conservative archbishop of Rio, Cardinal Jaime Camara, whom he would normally have succeeded. His friends, nuncio Lombardi and Pope Paul VI, looked for a suitable alternative. The first choice was Salvador, traditionally the primatial see, but the archbishop protested so furiously that the idea was dropped. A bull of appointment to São Luiz do Maranhão, a scenic colonial backwater, was drawn up, but then the archbishop of Olinda and Recife died suddenly, and the appointment was switched. Recife was both less distant from the centers of power and a political center in the Brazilian North-East, with a radical tradition. Its governor, Miguel Arraes, was a strong supporter of the Goulart government. On March 12, 1964, Helder Camara was named archbishop of Pernambuco's historic capital. Within weeks, on March 31, the military overthrew the civilian government.

---

9. José Oscar Beozzo, "Dom Helder Camara e o Concílio Vaticano II," unpublished lecture, Cuernavaca, 2002, published in an abridged version in Rocha, *Helder, o Dom*, 102–10.

Dom Helder initially tried to reduce the tension between the military and the socially active groups in the church, even meeting the new president, Humberto de Alencar Castelo Branco, before his move to Recife. His inaugural message to his new flock was in part a declaration of neutrality: "Let no one be shocked seeing me with individuals regarded as compromising and dangerous, from the left or the right, from the government or the opposition. Anti-reformists or reformists, anti-revolutionaries or revolutionaries, regarded as sincere or insincere. Let no one try to attach me to a group, link me to a party, try to make their friends my friends, or want me to adopt their feuds."

Aware of his travel commitments, since the Second Vatican Council still required his presence in Rome, Dom Helder launched into a frenzied round of meetings, with priests, religious, and lay organizations. To build a bridge with the elites, he organized a series of cultural nights in the archbishop's palace, on literature, sculpture, philosophy, and theology. The series concluded with a "Young People's Evening," in which the dining room became a dance floor. The unusual evening was a success — the only complaint: "There's not enough to drink and too many lights!"

For his ministry in the diocese, Dom Helder depended on a team of collaborators. The lynchpin of the system was his auxiliary bishop, José Lamartine, who managed the administration, a task for which Dom Helder had no particular talent. There were also episcopal vicars, for the clergy and for religious. The council of priests was given new importance. He delegated, partly because when he arrived in Recife, the Second Vatican Council was still in progress and required his presence in Rome, and he was receiving an increasing number of international invitations. He had agreed with the pope that he would limit his international journeys to four or five a year and a maximum period away from his diocese of two months, the vacation allowance for a bishop in canon law. Faithful to his ideal of a church of service and poverty, Dom Helder moved from the archbishop's palace to a two-room apartment at the back of a colonial church in downtown Recife. The core element of his pastoral strategy, "the apple of his eye," according to one of his episcopal vicars, was the "meetings of brothers and sisters," small group meetings in the community at which the participants discussed a talk broadcast by the archbishop. Each group had a leader, provided with a book containing the text of the talks and suggested questions, going from questions of faith to their implication in the life of the community. One group leader, Severina, formed five groups in a few weeks. This was the beginning of the base community system in the diocese.

For the task of humanitarian assistance and development, Dom Helder created Operation Hope, initially an appeal for donations to help victims of severe floods in June 1965. The program went on to provide training and employment. In 1971 it purchased sugar estates along the coast to the south of Recife to provide homes and employment for people with no other option.

At the height of the persecution mounted by the dictatorship the archbishop supported workers and students in their demands and protests and went himself to visit the families of those detained. Eventually this led to the creation of a Justice and Peace Commission, to investigate not only abuses of human rights such as illegal detention, but also the harm done by property speculation. The commission also had a role to educate the church in human rights and to help with the formation of organizations. "The political arm of the church," Dom Helder called it.

In response to demands from seminarians for a change in the system of training for the priesthood, a consultation was held to help the students assess the pros and cons of the seminary and possible alternatives: only 6 out of 147 voted for the seminary system. After extensive consultation with Rome, the seminary was closed and the students divided into groups living in the various communities of Olinda, with a team of tutors living in community in the house attached to the cathedral. To provide academic formation, the Recife Theological Institute, ITER, was set up, with staff, including women, from a range of disciplines

and open to lay people and religious as well as students for the
ordained ministry.

The archbishop's attempt at neutrality vis-à-vis the military
regime lasted three years, but after his repeated refusals to
join the celebrations for the anniversary of the military coup,
the local commander attacked him in the press. For almost
ten years, Dom Helder suffered unremitting harassment. He
was denounced in the press, bombs mysteriously exploded in
Recife, activists associated with the diocese were arrested, including Father Marcelo Cavalheira, later to become archbishop
of the neighboring diocese of João Pessoa. The worst moment
came in May 1969, when a young priest working as a chaplain
to students, Antonio Henrique Pereira, was brutally murdered.
There were rumors that Dom Helder was to be moved from Recife. Despite a machine-gun attack on the archbishop's palace,
the main pressures on Dom Helder were verbal, denunciations
in the media, including some by leading intellectuals. These
reached a climax in 1970, after Dom Helder had given examples of the torture of political prisoners at a mass meeting
in the Palais des Sports in Paris, in the presence of the archbishop, Cardinal Marty, and an estimated ten thousand people,
with as many more reported to be outside trying to get in.
Finally, an order was issued by the minister of justice ban-
ning "any references...favorable or hostile, to Dom Helder
Camara." To keep this media manipulation secret, the order
was not published: officers took copies, showed them to editors,
and then took them away again. Even to attack the archbishop
would give him publicity: it was better that he should disappear,
become a non-person.

Fortunately he had the continued support of Pope Paul VI:
"Any act of yours, any remark, echoes round the world. It's
more important for the European and North American press to
know what you think than to know the views of any cardinal,
even a North American.... You have grown internally, but you
are still as humble as the near-seminarist I met in 1950. Your
smile and your look do not age.... Take advantage of this fame.
Without ceasing to be the pastor of Olinda and Recife — and,

thank God, you have a pastor's soul — remember that there are few in the church whose voice deserves a hearing as much as yours."[10] His old friend reaffirmed his support at their last meeting, six weeks before the pope's death in August 1978.

One of Dom Helder's worst moments was when doubt was cast on the pope's support in the form of a letter from the Vatican secretary of state, Cardinal Benelli, which reached him shortly after the murder of Father Antonio Henrique, talking about the "difficulties" his statements could cause outside his diocese and the need for "deepening of faith to keep pace with social involvement." "It was like being stabbed in the heart," Dom Helder exclaimed. These letters continued to come, even as Paul VI continued to assure Dom Helder when they met that he supported his foreign travels. Even the leaders of the Brazilian bishops conference insisted on being informed of his travel plans. Fortunately, a group of fellow bishops consistently supported him, including Paulo Evaristo Arns, archbishop of São Paulo since 1970. Arns and Camara became close friends, inventing a relationship of "uncle" and "nephew" — modeled, according to Dom Helder, on the pope's relationship of father to his sons, the bishops. When Arns challenged the military regime in 1975 by opening his cathedral for an interfaith service for the Jewish journalist Wladimir Herzog, Dom Helder made a discreet appearance and advised the younger man on how to avoid problems as the congregation dispersed.

The Brazilian military dictatorship used its embassy in Oslo and its contacts with Norwegian investors in Brazil to prevent the award of the Nobel Peace Prize to Dom Helder, who nonetheless was nominated for the award on three occasions. In compensation, Norwegian churches and NGOs awarded him a "People's Peace Prize" in 1974, one of twenty-one international awards and eighteen degrees that testified to the esteem in which he was held by the international community.

It was not until 1980 that Dom Helder could again speak openly to his own people through the media, and by then he

---

10. Piletti and Praxedes, *Dom Helder Camara*, 359.

had only fours years left before the age of seventy-five, at which
bishops are obliged to submit their resignation to the pope.
Now the Polish pope, John Paul II, was governing the Roman
Catholic Church, and there was no longer the same tolerance
for experiments in church structures and aspirations toward socialism, however humanized. Though on his visit to Recife in
July 1980 the pope acclaimed him as "brother of the poor and
my brother!" no account was taken of his preferences as regards his successor. Dom Helder retired officially on July 15,
1985, and was promptly replaced by Dom José Cardoso, a little
known canon lawyer. What followed was a systematic disman-
tling of the structures Dom Helder had put in place. The Justice
and Peace Commission was abolished and its premises subsequently sold off for the construction of a shopping mall. The
Theological Institute was closed, and the old seminary high up
near Olinda's colonial heart was reopened.

Dom Helder refused to make any comment on his successor's policies and devoted himself to the foundation he had set
up to promote development projects, including a campaign for
"A Year 2000 without Poverty." While his successor, Dom José,
kept a low public profile, Dom Helder, until his death in 1999,
remained in demand in Recife to lend prestige to occasions of
all sorts, and he was warmly celebrated on the occasion of significant anniversaries, including his eightieth birthday in 1989
and his sixty-five years as a priest in 1996. But the great communicator had fallen silent. Many years earlier, in words that in
retrospect seem sadly prescient, the great archbishop had said:

> I'm not preoccupied with death. My motto, the motto of
> my life and my episcopacy, is *In manus tuas,* "Into Thy
> Hands." The Lord protects me so well that I can deliver
> myself with absolute trust into his fatherly hands. But I do
> still ask myself: 'How will my sister death come to me?'
> What I find most difficult to accept, but I do accept it, is
> the possibility that the Lord may choose to let me survive
> myself, I mean, to let my body survive my mind. When
> I first went to Rio de Janeiro people still talked about

Cardinal Arcoverde, the first Brazilian and Latin American cardinal. He had been a great bishop, but at the end of his life he became a child again, you know.... It isn't easy to accept the idea of surviving like that. But I do accept in advance even that form of death.

I continue with my work: but all the time I am quietly and calmly preparing to receive the death the Lord intends for me.[11]

Conclusion

This anthology draws almost entirely on material published in English. It does not claim to offer a comprehensive analysis of Helder Camara's thought. For that it would be necessary to re-search the archive of his speeches and meditations now assembled in the Instituto Dom Helder Camara in Recife. The first publication from the archive, a volume of Dom Helder's letters from the Second Vatican Council, was published in Recife in 2004.

Nevertheless this sampling of the ideas of Helder Camara recovers the message of a Christian leader undeservedly forgotten. Among the points of interest are Dom Helder's development from a conservative and authoritarian form of Catholicism to a conviction that liberty is at the heart of the Christian Gospel, a liberty based on the boundless love of the Creator. This led him to take up radical positions on church discipline and structures and to develop a positive attitude toward other faiths and belief systems. In the universal church, this attitude was exemplified in the effervescence around Vatican II. Today, in many ways, we see a church whose leaders are trying to row back from that position. Nevertheless, despite prohibitions and censure, inquiry into the relationship of Christianity with other faiths continues. Another aspect of Dom Helder's thought, his relationship with nature and his sense of the unity of creation, an attitude coming from deep within his being and also perhaps influenced by

---

11. Camara, *The Conversions of a Bishop*, 215–16.

St. Francis of Assisi, feeds the hunger felt today by those who feel that the dominant trends in spirituality have had a sort of tunnel vision in relation to humankind's place in nature and have even encouraged a predatory attitude to the rest of the natural world.

OTHER WORKS CONSULTED

By Dom Helder Camara

English

Hoping against All Hope. Maryknoll, N.Y.: Orbis Books, 1984.
Into Your Hands, Lord. Bloomington, Ind.: Meyer-Stone, 1987.
Questions for Living. Maryknoll, N.Y.: Orbis Books, 1987.
Race against Time. New York: Dimension, 1971.
Revolution through Peace. New York: Harper & Row, 1971.
Spiral of Violence. New York: Dimension, 1971.
A Thousand Reasons for Living. Philadelphia: Fortress, 1981.
A Voice of the Third World. New York: Paulist, 1972.

Portuguese

Nossa Senhora no meu caminho. São Paulo: Edições Paulinas, 1981.
Um olhar sobre a cidade (1995). Radio talks from 1982.
Opção pelos pobres: Educação e nova sociedade. Camara, Arns, and others. São Paulo, 1983.
Rosas para meu Deus. São Paulo: Edições Paulinas, 1996.
Vaticano II: Correspondência conciliar. Vol. 1. Recife, 2004.

About Dom Helder Camara

de Castro, Marcos. *Dom Helder: Misticismo e santidade.* Rio de Janeiro: Civilização Brasileira, 2002.
Hall, Mary. *The Impossible Dream: The Spirituality of Dom Helder Camara.* Maryknoll, N.Y.: Orbis Books, 1980.
Piletti, Nelson, and Walter Práxedes. *Dom Helder Camara: Entre o poder e a profecia.* São Paulo: Editora Atica, 1997.
Rocha, Zildo , ed. *Helder, o Dom: Uma vida que marcou os rumos da Igreja no Brasil.* 3rd ed. Petrópolis: Vozes, 2000. Essays by friends and colleagues.

1

A Church of Service and Poverty

Dom Helder's understanding of the church was profoundly influenced by the Second Vatican Council, in which he was an active participant, though he never made a speech in the plenary sessions. Crucial to the Council's work was the input of scholars in every field of theology and church life, discussed by pastors from the whole range of cultures that make up the universal church. Dom Helder actively promoted these discussions through the weekly lectures he organized at the Brazilian bishops' residence, the Domus Mariae. He brought to the process the experience of dealing with the challenges presented to the church in a rapidly changing world, first through his work with Catholic Action in Brazil, then through his role in setting up the Brazilian bishops conference, and finally his involvement in the Latin American Episcopal Council, CELAM, which sought to coordinate the work of the church across the whole continent. For Dom Helder and a like-minded minority of bishops the aim of the renewal was to enable the church to engage more effectively with "the joys and hopes... of the people of this age," as the Council's document on the church in the modern world put it, and in particular the gulf between the rich and poor worlds. The other reforms, of the liturgy, of clerical dress, and so on, the endorsement of ecumenism, the recognition of human rights, were for him means to this end. By doing this, he argued, the church would come closer to the spirit and practice of its founder. For Dom Helder, the church needed to become a

*"church of service and poverty," leaving behind the attitudes of
the sixteenth-century Counter-Reformation.*

*Perhaps the core theme that runs through the selections
reproduced in this chapter is the indivisible unity between
preaching the Gospel and promoting human development. At
the same time, far from reducing the church's work to social
work or political activism, Dom Helder presents it as a response
to a deep faith in the presence of Christ in the poor and the in-
spiration of the Holy Spirit in work for human betterment. As
with Archbishop Romero and Thomas Merton, Dom Helder's
engagement in politics is an extension of his mysticism.*

DOM HELDER INTRODUCES HIMSELF
TO THE PEOPLE OF OLINDA AND RECIFE

*Dom Helder's first message to his new diocese in 1964 is an
eloquent statement of his view of the church and the role of
the bishop: one of service to all, irrespective of creed. The new
archbishop also proclaimed his special concern for the poor and
expressed in dramatic terms his theological conviction that in
the poor we meet Christ: "in the North-East Christ is called
Zé, Antônio, Severino." In working for development we are
bringing relief to the suffering Christ.*

*But the message was also extremely political. Dom Helder
was speaking less than two weeks after the military seized
power and in a city that was a center of radical political and
social activity. He was walking a tightrope, hoping not to alien-
ate the military while defending key demands of the radicals:
"basic reforms" was a slogan of the government that had just
been overthrown. Charity was not enough: what was required
was development and justice, but now that the military coup
had removed the danger of communism, it was safe to proceed
with reforms: "Without detriment to national security measures
and the alert against communism, let us not denounce as communists those who merely hunger and thirst for social justice
and Brazil's development."*

The text reproduced here consists of key passages from the message.

Who am I and who am I talking to and who do I wish to talk to?

A North-Easterner talking to North-Easterners, with my eyes fixed on Brazil, Latin America, the world. A human creature who considers himself a brother in weakness and sin to the people of all races and all corners of the world. A Christian addressing Christians, but with a heart open, ecumenically, to people of all creeds and all ideologies. A bishop of the Catholic Church who, in imitation of Christ, does not come to be served, but to serve.

Catholics or non-Catholics, believers or unbelievers, hear my brotherly greeting: Praised be our Lord Jesus Christ.

Let no one be scandalized when they see me with individuals regarded as unworthy or sinful. Who is not a sinner? Asked about sinners, Jesus replied that it was precisely the sick that need a doctor.

Let no one be shocked seeing me with individuals regarded as compromising and dangerous, from the left or the right, from the government or the opposition. Anti-reformists or reformists, anti-revolutionaries or revolutionaries, regarded as sincere or insincere.

Let no one try to attach me to a group, link me to a party, try to make their friends my friends or want me to adopt their feuds.

My door and my heart will be open to all, to absolutely all. Christ died for all people: I must exclude no one from brotherly dialogue.

A Special Love for the Poor

Obviously, while I love all, I must, like Christ, have a special love for the poor. At the last judgment, we shall all be judged by the treatment we have given to Christ, to Christ in the person of those who are hungry or thirsty, who are dirty, wounded, and oppressed.

Continuing the activities to which our archdiocese already devotes itself, we shall care for the poor, with special concern for shameful poverty, and trying to prevent poverty sliding into destitution. Poverty can and sometimes should be a gift generously accepted or even spontaneously offered to the Father. Destitution is revolting and degrading: it wounds the image of God in every human being; it violates every human being's right and duty to achieve all-round perfection.

Of course, the slums and abandoned children have a special place in our thoughts.

Anyone who is suffering, in body or soul, anyone, poor or rich, who is in despair, will have a special place in the bishop's heart.

Charity Is Not Enough

But I have not come to help anyone to delude themselves by thinking that all we need is a little generosity and social work. Of course, there are cases of shocking poverty to which we have no right to remain indifferent. Very often, we have to give immediate assistance. But don't let us think that the problem is limited to a few minor reforms, and let us not confuse the beautiful and essential idea of order, the goal of all human progress, with impoverished versions of it that are responsible for keeping in place structures that we all recognize cannot be retained.

If we want to get to the roots of our social problems, we will have to help the country to break the vicious circle of underdevelopment and destitution. Some people are scandalized when they are told that this is our number one social problem. Some people think of demagogy when we talk about people living in subhuman situations....

But development can't be implemented top down; it can't be imposed. Let us not be afraid of correct ideas even if they are often misused: development implies an awakening of minds, an awakening of public feeling, an awakening of culture, self-advancement, technical planning....

The church does not stay at the edge of history. It lives at the heart of history through its free, adult, and responsible laity.

The Church Cannot Abandon the People

I would like anyone who is shocked by the line this message is taking, anyone worried by the bishop's ideas and language, to come with me on this train of thought.

Let us have spiritual serenity and Christian courage to rescue correct ideas embodied in expressions that at this moment sound almost like banned, ugly words. "Popular culture," "conscientization," "politicization," "self-advancement" may perhaps be words we should forget for a while or even replace, but we cannot abandon correct ideals simply because they have fallen into the wrong hands. How can we fear movements concerned with genuine democracy, which can only be successful in regimes that respect freedom! How can we fear movements that are in essence deeply Christian?

It would be scandalous and unforgivable for the masses to be abandoned by the church in their darkest hour. It would give the impression that the church had no interest in helping them to reach a level of human and Christian dignity and rise to the status of a people.

We all believe that all human beings are children of the same heavenly Father. Those who have the same father are brothers and sisters. Let us really treat each other as brothers and sisters!

We all believe that God made man in his own image and likeness and charged him with dominating the earth and completing creation. Let us do all we can to ensure that in the North-East all work is work in which the creature feels that he or she is helping the Creator to build the world.

We all believe that freedom is a divine gift to be preserved at all costs. Let us liberate, in the highest and most profound sense of the word, all the human beings who live round about us.

The church does not wish to dominate the course of events. It wishes to serve human beings by helping them in their liberation. And it will be present to say that this liberation, while it begins in time, will reach its complete fulfillment only when the Son of God returns at the end of time, which is the true beginning.

Working for Development Is Serving Christ

Let us speed up, wasting no time, as a Christian act, an act of evangelization, the enterprise of development. It will do us no good if we venerate beautiful images of Christ. I will go further: it is still not enough if we stop before the poor person and recognize in them the disfigured face of the Savior, if we do not identify Christ with the human creature to be dragged out of underdevelopment.

Strange as it may seem to some, I declare that in the North-East Christ is called Zé, Antônio, Severino. *Ecce homo:* here is Christ, here is humanity. He is the person who needs justice, who has a right to justice, who deserves justice....

In our country everyone understands and declares that basic reforms cannot be postponed. Many people had suspicions about those who were carrying out the reforms, and especially fear of communist infiltration. Now that the situation has changed, we have no time to waste. The long-awaited reforms must come without delay. They may be just and balanced, but on no account can they seem to be an illusion.

Let the reforms come without need for coercion and above all without conflicts and bitterness. May the Brazilian people be increasingly incapable of hate and realize that this is really the great, the greatest sin, non-love, because God is charity: God is love.

And as for the North-East, as, through defeats and hopes, it begins to rise into development, may it give to all Brazil the example of dynamic peace based on justice, of truth in charity, of brotherly dialogue and understanding, beyond the divisions that could drag the country into civil war and chaos.

May the North-East send out right across Brazil the example of rapid recovery from the political crisis from which we are emerging. Without detriment to national security measures and the alert against communism, let us not denounce as communists those who merely hunger and thirst for social justice and Brazil's development.

May the North-East help Brazil not to cheat the people's hopes. Let us prove that democracy is able to get to the roots of our problems.

— Translated from the original Portuguese
of Dom Helder's inaugural sermon, 1964

OPENING PEOPLE'S EYES

A key phase in Dom Helder's development and in the radicalization of the Brazilian church was his time as national chaplain to Catholic Action. This was an organization, launched in 1927, intended to encourage lay Catholics to apply the principles of their faith to society. It had specialized branches: in the English-speaking world the best known are probably the Young Christian Workers and the Young Christian Students. It had a radical potential deriving from the methodology of one of its leaders, Joseph Cardijn: "See, Judge, and Act," in other words: look at what's happening, analyze it, and do something about it. In the social ferment that was Brazil in the 1950s, this could be dynamite. Dom Helder's initial contribution was to establish a coordinated national organization, based on a secretariat in the then capital of Brazil, Rio de Janeiro. As he notes, it foreshadowed the structure of the later National Conference of Brazilian Bishops.

From the beginning the secretariat enabled us to keep in touch with the whole country. We had the support of all the bishops connected with Catholic Action, as well as the cardinal of Rio and the new cardinal of São Paulo, Vasconcelos Motta. We also had the support of the papal nuncio, Monsignor Chiarlo. So even before the National Conference of Bishops was founded we were able to begin organizing the regional meetings of bishops, which I told you about before, and to discover some of the major problems of the people.

At the same time, in Brazil as in other countries, the "special" branches of Catholic Action were developing. The general Catholic Action organization was opening people's eyes to human problems; but specialized Catholic Action went much further: it took us right into the midst of the workers, peasants, students, and so on, operating on the basis of Cardijn's trilogy — see, judge, act. Long before the phrase was invented, we were busy with the task of "consciousness raising."

Of course we had problems. As soon as the privileged classes, those who exploit the people, see that they have been found out, they begin to murmur until they accuse us outright: "But you're changing religion! You're changing the church! The church has always been our friend. But now you're turning it against us! You're teaching people to hate the rich!"

One of the problems in Brazil is that the hierarchy of the church has a rather...curious attitude to politics. When it's a matter of politics in the general sense of the word, in aid of the common good, they say it is the Christian's duty to become involved as the Gospel requires us to do. But at the same time the church itself is afraid of becoming involved in party politics or taking any stand against the government or the established order.

That doesn't take account of the fact that if you are not on the side of the oppressed you are on the side of the oppressors. It is always very difficult to remain neutral. And in our case — particularly in the regions and sectors where injustice is most flagrant — neutrality is really impossible. Of course we have to be very careful that in bringing about the advancement of the oppressed we don't encourage them to imitate the only kind of advancement they have ever seen — to follow the example set by their oppressors. It's very tempting and very easy — as many so-called revolutions have demonstrated — to transform the oppressed into oppressors. It's far more difficult to denounce and combat injustice without preaching hatred and becoming full of hatred yourself.

But you have to understand that young people are very logical, very genuine. They aren't bothered about prudence, or nuances, or precautions. It's only normal for young people to be radical. Too often people forget their own youth. When the bishops and the priests and the padres get the young people together and show them the great encyclicals and the conclusions reached at the Second Vatican Council or at Medellín, the young people think these encyclicals and conclusions are meant to be put into practice. They can't understand why these wonderful ideas have to go through some long, slow process before they can be applied. Fortunately, young people reject all this false prudence — which I'm sure Christ himself is the first to reject. But it's the human weakness of the Everlasting Church.

As time went on certain members of the hierarchy became obsessed with what they saw as the Marxist tendencies of the university groups and the student groups. I don't condemn anyone for it: I know the bishops were sincere. But that's the way it always is. If you take the encyclical *Populorum Progressio* and try to put it into practice, you are a Marxist....

My God! Marxism!...And Medellín?...In 1968 we held a meeting at Medellín in Colombia of bishops representing all the episcopal conferences of Latin America. You couldn't imagine a more official sort of meeting. It had been called by the pope. It had been officially opened by him in Bogotá, at the end of the International Eucharistic Congress. And when the assembly moved from Bogotá to Medellín three personal representatives of the Holy Father remained with us. We delegates had either been elected by our episcopal conferences, or we had been nominated by the pope. All of the resolutions had been freely discussed and passed by vote. Every word and sentence of the document had been examined in Rome. Everything had been approved. Even our denunciation of internal colonialism, in other words the colonialism that is practiced within our country and our continent by privileged groups who maintain their wealth by keeping their compatriots in misery and poverty. Even our denunciation of structural injustice, in other words injustice that arises not just occasionally or accidentally, but structurally, and can be abolished only by changing social structures. Even our decision not just to preach the ideal of education as a liberating force, but to put it into practice. All of this was there, in the official documents produced by the conference, for everyone to read; and young people read them.

But we didn't have the right to be naive. We were grown men, bishops, ministers. We had experts with us, highly qualified advisers. We knew that the privileged classes couldn't listen to all of this without reacting. A reaction was inevitable, obvious. It was bound to come.

And when it came it was intelligently done. The privileged classes are very reluctant to attack the church. They have enormous respect for the pope. They are loyal to the true church and are the true, the only defenders of Christian civilization. And it was love of the church, simply love of the church, that prompted them to denounce the Marxist infiltration that was gnawing at its heart.... Because clearly all this talk of oppressors and oppressed was Marxist-inspired; the idea of denouncing internal colonialism could have come only from Moscow; the desire to put an end to structural injustice is nothing but Maoism. Clearly!

How can I explain it?... It's true that the church has always been a friend and ally of the rich. On the great *fazendas* [plantations] in Brazil there was always a church and a chaplain. And now suddenly the church had become a problem. But no, it wasn't possible. It couldn't be the church: it must be something else. It must be Marxist infiltration among the students, among the nuns and the priests, and even among the bishops!

On one occasion — after 1964, I'm not sure exactly when — a delegation of women came to see the papal nuncio, Monsignor Lombardi. They had come to present him with a list of bishops tainted with Marxism, whom they wanted him to transfer or even dismiss entirely. They began to read the names on the list. But after the first name Monsignor Lombardi — he was a very fine nuncio — stopped them. "Forgive me, ladies. Don't you think you have said enough? I can't listen to you any more. The first name is enough to tell me that I needn't know any more. Please excuse me."

Nevertheless some members of the hierarchy believed — and there are some who still believe today — that the church really was being infiltrated by Marxists. — CB, 115–19

THE IDEA OF A BISHOPS CONFERENCE

The world secretary for the Holy Year was Monsignor Pignedoli. Monsignor Pignedoli invited me back to Rome at the end of 1950 for a meeting of all the national secretaries. The first World Conference of the Laity was being held at the same time, and I was asked to prepare the Brazilian contribution to the conference. The program covered a number of different themes, and we prepared a paper on each one. But I remember each paper ended with the same conclusion: "None of this will be possible or effective until there is a national conference of bishops in Brazil."

Until the beginning of this century there was a very small number of dioceses in Brazil. And then in a matter of a few years the Holy See decided to increase the number of dioceses and bishops. Now when a priest is appointed bishop and entrusted with a diocese he immediately comes up against all sorts of different and complex problems. He hasn't time to come to Rio de Janeiro: the country is too vast, the distances too great. He has no one to help him. When I thought of a national conference, I envisaged a national secretariat as well which would serve all the bishops of the church of Christ incarnate in this land of Brazil. — CB, 131, 133–34

THE "CHURCH OF THE POOR" AT VATICAN II

I am very fond of that name, which comes from our French brethren: "The Church of Poverty and Service." The Holy Spirit

has called us and brought us together. He has opened our eyes
to the duty of Christians, but especially of pastors, to imitate Christ, who although he belonged to all people, identified
himself with the poor, the oppressed, and all those who suffered. We have begun to look for a way of making the whole
church, but first of all each one of us individually "poor and a
servant."

As I have already told you, I didn't realize at that time that
true poverty is not the kind we choose but the kind that God
sends. I thought for instance that the clothes I wore could be a
sign of poverty. But when the photographers used to follow me
everywhere, I realized that external poverty is worthless unless
it is a manifestation of internal poverty. There is a real danger
of pride in humility: "Look at me! I am a poor bishop, a bishop
of the poor! I am not like those bourgeois bishops." That is
terrible. You see it wasn't until later that I knew that the poverty
God had chosen for me was not to take away wealth — which
in any case I didn't have — but to snatch away my fame, my
reputation, my prestige.

The churchmen in this country and in this continent used to
be so preoccupied with upholding authority and the social order
that we were incapable of seeing the terrible injustices that
were and still are perpetuated by this so-called social order. The
Christianity we preached was too passive: patience, obedience,
acceptance of suffering in union with Christ. Great virtues, of
course: but in the context they merely reinforced oppression.
And during all this time, the governments and the great land-
lords were pleased and proud that the church guaranteed them
this support.

But when we opened our eyes to the brutal reality, after the
social encyclicals, the Second Vatican Council and Medellín,
it became impossible for us to continue in the same way. It
came as a great surprise to the proprietors of the established
order when their traditional ally, the church, turned against
them. More and more Catholic laymen, priests, nuns, and even
bishops began to denounce the injustices — at least, the most se-

rious injustices — in Brazil. According to the theory of national
security, this makes them agitators and subversives. And we
have to accept the consequences.   — *CB*, 198

THE COURAGE TO REFORM

The liturgical revival...had a profound effect on us. And so
did the biblical revival. They helped us to a better spiritual
understanding of the Ecumenical Council....I should explain
perhaps that we are only now beginning to have the courage to
allow ourselves, for instance, a certain degree of liturgical creativity. We always used to think, we priests and bishops, that
nothing must be changed, not even the rubrics. The rubrics were
sacred! I remember how we were taught to arrange our fingers
during Mass, after the consecration. That was sacred, too! And
when a bishop was about to administer communion, the body
of Christ, the communicant would first of all have to kiss his
ring. Imagine that: first the ring, then the body of Christ! It
was as if the respect due to the bishop and the communion service were placed on the same level of importance as the love of
Christ!

It's only now that we are beginning to have a little more
courage in introducing reforms. This is unfortunately one of
the human weaknesses of the church: the confusion between
the prudence of the Holy Spirit and the prudence of the flesh,
human prudence. Under the influence of the Holy Spirit we
may have remarkable courage for composing fine resolutions
and drawing large conclusions. But afterward we are tempted
by prudence: "We must be patient." And what happens is that
while the commissioners in Rome are busy making up rules
and regulations for our lives, the young seminarians, the new
priests, the laity, the people and Christian communities, go on
ahead, far, far ahead. If the advocates of prudence and patience
were to take a trip around the world, they'd get an enormous
shock. You can't regulate the Holy Spirit!   — *CB*, 98–99

We must not allow our house to be called a palace, and we must take care that it really is not one. There is a theory that can be historically proved: before undertaking reforms in depth, the church has always had to come to terms with poverty. Let us take the initiative and suppress our personal titles of Eminence, Beatitude, Excellency. Let us lose the mania of considering ourselves nobles, and let us renounce our coats of arms and heraldic devices. Let us simplify our attire. Let us not have our moral force and authority depend upon the make of our car. Let us pay serious attention to our place of residence.

Important as all this is, it concerns our outer aspect, one might say. The essential thing is our mentality. Let us have the courage to examine our conscience and our life. Have we or have we not adopted a capitalistic mentality, do we or do we not employ methods and proceedings quite suitable to bankers but not very suitable to a representative of Christ?

Providence has already delivered us from the Papal States. When will the hour of God come that will bring the church back to rejoin Lady Poverty?

We "Excellencies" need an excellent reform. We have had enough of a church that wants to be served and demands to be always the first served; a church that lacks the humility and realism to accept the condition of religious pluralism; a church that proclaims "in season and out of season" (2 Tim. 4:2) that she has a monopoly on truth. Enough of prince-bishops who keep themselves at a distance from the people and even from the clergy!   — VP, 5

WE CANNOT ACCEPT A MUSEUM-CHURCH

I'm not a textual critic. I don't propose to argue over this passage (Matt. 22:15–22). I know there are plenty of other sayings of Jesus helping us to grasp the totality of what he meant to say, not merely throwing light on a part of it. I also know that the church goes on being the living presence of Christ. With all respect for what the Lord said in the days of the apostles, I try to keep alert and catch what he's saying today. And I sense that Christ does not intend to separate, to set up an antithesis between God and human beings, spiritual values and temporal realities, eternity and our duties of today. Eternity begins here and now. Here and now we're building it.

During my life as a priest and bishop, I have seen and experienced several kinds of relationship between what used to be called "the two swords": the temporal power and the spiritual power, state and church. At one point I even thought we in Brazil had struck an ideal balance of relations, based on mutual respect and effective cooperation. The chariot of the church and the chariot of the state advanced in tandem, solidly linked together. And this with the best intentions in the world, since we thought we could work together like this in the service of our people.

But today I am calmly convinced that the church's only engagement and solidarity should be with the people. If the government too becomes engaged with the people, then a fruitful meeting between government and church can take place at this level.

But governments, whether of right or left, who claim they wish to serve the people, do not care to meet the church with the people. They are happy enough to load the church with honors and privileges, provided it stays inside its churches, praising God with lovely services — provided it doesn't meddle in current problems. Economic, social, political problems are Earth's business, not the Kingdom of Heaven's!

We cannot accept this position, the role of a museum-church. It isn't a question of reclaiming power or of seeking to recover the prestige that goes with that power. It's a question of doing our brotherly, or sisterly, duty by our fellow beings under ordeal, suffering, being crushed. We are responsible for being brother or sister to all people without stopping to consider whether we're dealing with Catholics or Christians or believers. Enough for us to know that every human creature is our brother or our sister, the child of the same Father.

— *TTG*, 130–32

THE ROLE OF THE PAPACY

It doesn't shock me to encounter human weakness in the papacy: the first pope was himself all too human. Remarkable for some of his responses, impressive in his dreams about loving Christ — "even if all the others desert you." ... But weak. In the Garden of Gethsemane he slept. When the soldiers arrived he drew his sword. When the servants asked him if he was with Jesus, he didn't want to know him any more.

How well I understand Peter. He's our brother and no mistake. The popes are Peter's brothers. Obviously they have a special charism, but they're human creatures prone to weakness nonetheless.

Pope Alexander VI Borgia was weak, weak, weak in his personal life. But when the moment came for acting as the successor of Peter, he safeguarded what was essential. The Holy Spirit was there.

I like this man Peter. He's very much one of us. I shouldn't have liked all the popes always to be holy and perfect. Once we human creatures become convinced we cannot fall, we soon find we can't understand other people's weaknesses anymore. By allowing us to fall, into the mud if need be, the Lord preserves us in humility. In one of the psalms it says, "You are good because you have humbled us."

The Lord made Peter, so weak and so humble, the chief of the apostles. But in the course of history, the church of the apostles split apart. And we have come a long way now in our divisions. I remember how in the seminary people used to speak of Luther and the other reformers. Today, I'm glad to see, we are having to re-evaluate the figure of Luther. He was a prophet, in his way. He denounced the scandalous abuses at Rome and in the church. During the Council and on the three occasions when I met John XXIII, I thought, "If only Luther, still remaining Luther but capable of reasonable discussion as well, had found himself with a John XXIII, we might perhaps have avoided the scandal of schism."

Efforts are being made everywhere now to reconcile our differences. When I was a boy, priests were still burning Protestant Bibles. Today we have the same books, the same texts and, very often, especially when times are bad, we pray and work together. But the divisions have lasted so long and gone so deep that our peoples don't always understand each other even now.

For me, you know, the pope is truly Peter. He's been chosen by the Lord to be, in a very special way, the sign of unity. The pope works for ecumenism. — *TTG,* 95–96

I like these little details: the Lord had already lit the fire, ready to cook the fish (John 21:4–12). The Lord is just as considerate after his resurrection as before. . . . I love God's delicacy of touch. And another detail: after Jesus died, after Jesus was dead, here's Peter, supposed to be the prince of the apostles, the first pope — naked, trying to fish! I love the simplicity of it.

Why have we made things so complicated? Why haven't we stayed simple like Christ and his disciples?

It isn't only the pope's fault; it's much more our own fault if the pope can't be simple like Peter. We bishops, we Christians are mainly responsible for this. It's terribly hard being pope.

One day Pope John said to me, "Oh, yes, this needs doing. That needs doing. . . . "

Then he went on, "but I shan't be able to get it done."

"But, Father, I've been taught since I was so high that the pope has the power to do anything."

"Huh! If you were in my shoes, you'd know I've got eight people telling me what *not* to do."

There you have it: we tell the popes what *not* to do. If we encouraged them instead, they would take simplicity even further, which is what they want to do. I'm sure this is what they want to do. But it isn't easily done.

We must do what we can to liberate the pope, liberate the bishops, liberate Christ's church. And the Gospel goes on to tell how Christ did with Peter what he loves doing with us too. He still asks us the same question: "Do you love me?" The first time we hear it, our hearts quake with joy, with bliss. Then the Lord insists, "Do you really love me?" The reason why he repeats the question a third time is because he knows how weak we are. Because of our weakness, he knows we may even be capable of wanting to offend him. He wants to preserve us from that.

I have always dreamed of seeing the pope, Peter's successor, the supreme representative of Christ, traveling about like a pastor, encouraging and fortifying his brethren. This was the mission that the Lord entrusted Peter with: "I prayed for thee so that when thou hast overcome temptation thou canst help thy brethren, and encourage them."

But the Vatican State remains an anomaly. I understand of course that the sovereignty of the little Vatican State helps to ensure the independence of the pope and the government of the church, but it causes dreadful anomalies. The pope tries enormously hard to travel like a simple pastor, but he is always received like a head of state. And it's just awful. I was at the airport when Paul VI arrived at Bogotá. All you could see was soldiers, soldiers, soldiers — with machine-guns — all the way from the airport to his residence. I have no wish to see the pope come to Brazil under these conditions, protected by machine-guns.... I long for the day when the pope will really be just a bishop, the president of the synod of bishops, the chief link in the collegiality of bishops, the head of God's people, and no longer a king.... Then he will be able to travel without worrying about security and about risking his life.

I know that the popes themselves — particularly the last ones, John XXIII and Paul VI, are the ones who suffer most from the errors of the past. It's obvious that they personally would prefer to be pastors rather than heads of state. I once saw something on television that made me very happy. Paul VI was being received at the United Nations with great ceremony by representatives from all the nations of the world. But he behaved so naturally! He came in, took off his cape by himself and gave it to someone, and sat down. He behaved just like an ordinary human being, just as if he were Peter himself, or Paul.

Oh, when will we manage to help the church of Christ to liberate itself! If we're going to help to liberate the world we must work to liberate the pope, and the bishops and all Christians.
— *CB*, 159–60

Every majority is the expression of an active minority. In every human group, and therefore in episcopal conferences as well, the Holy Spirit moves a minority. If there is a problem, it is this minority that faces it. It has to be careful of two things.

First, it must not impose its point of view on the rest. It should explain its principles clearly; but at the same time it must make it clear that it has no wish to impose those principles on others. It needs to convince, not to vanquish.

Second, it must enact the principles it preaches, and enact them humbly. The active minority is no more intelligent, no more shrewd, no more human or no more holy than the rest. Pharisaism is a deadly temptation: without humility and without love....

But there are minorities at work, not in just one or two episcopal conferences, but in conferences all over the world, even in Rome. We have to understand what the Holy Spirit tells us through the Gospel and through the entire history of the church up to the last Council. We need a minority in the Vatican that can understand and enact not only episcopal collegiality but also co-responsibility in the church of the Lord; that can understand and enact the primacy of the pope in terms of service and love, and only in terms of service and love: that is essential for ecumenism; that can understand and enact the Roman Curia not as a kind of superstate, but as an instrument to serve all of God's people, in other words to serve the whole of the church, and not just the pope and the hierarchy.

And it won't be long, it won't be long.   — *CB*, 144–45

TRUE EVANGELIZATION

People will always argue the respective merits of "horizontalism" and "verticalism," of "evangelization" and "humanization." I'm certain the Lord doesn't see these as separate, still less as mutually opposed. God's history and human history are interwoven. They proceed together.

Personally speaking, I could never confine myself solely to "evangelization." For some years, as you know, the authorities in my country prohibited me from appearing on television. At a given moment, I was informed I might speak on TV again if I stuck strictly to evangelization. I replied that as far as I was concerned it would be absolutely impossible for me to draw the line. To those who waste their time discussing the respective merits of "horizontalism" and "verticalism," I always say: neither the horizontal line alone, nor the vertical line alone, can form a cross. To have a proper cross, you have to have both the horizontal and the vertical. The horizontal line is the arms of Christ spread wide to all humanity's huge problems.

Oh, I don't care for those representations of Christ on the cross where he has his arms above his head. I like to see him with his arms wide open, since this is how I always meet him, always ready to accept and bear all the facts of human life. The Passion still goes on. I touch, I encounter the Passion every minute of my life. And Christ is there, with open arms.

— *TTG*, 131

CLERGY AND LAITY

In this discussion Dom Helder is reflecting on the changes made in priestly formation in his diocese and the other dioceses of the region in the 1960s and 1970s, and his insistence that the laity should have leadership roles. These changes were reversed by his successor, and the seminary system was restored. Though now periods of helping in parishes are part of the students' preparation, there is no longer support for the bold experiments undertaken by the Brazilian bishops in this period. A structure that has survived more widely in Latin America is that of the base communities or "grassroots communities," as they are called elsewhere in the world — groups of Christians in the neighborhood, engaged in reflection, worship, and action.

The Seminary

In my day there was a junior seminary and a senior seminary. Sometimes boys went to a preseminary school first. And sometimes they went to a holiday seminary. In other words, from early childhood until his ordination the future priest was protected, protected, protected. And then one day suddenly he found himself free, without any preparation for freedom or any idea how to deal with it.

It's odd: in those days, when I was in the seminary, we thought it perfectly normal that we should prepare ourselves to serve the people by keeping our distance from them for years and years. Eleven, twelve, thirteen years....

Today it isn't like that any more. That's also odd: there are times when you know the Holy Spirit is moving among us. If something changes in a particular place, in a specific town, district, or village, you may think it's the result of an idea, or the actions, of an individual or group, or a current fashion. But when it's the same idea and attitude that springs up at more or less the same time, here, there, and everywhere — all over — then you know it's the breath of the Holy Spirit. And that was how it was: suddenly the young men who wanted to be priests felt that the best way of preparing themselves to serve the people was to remain among them. A novice today simply wouldn't dream of going and shutting himself up in an institution for years and years.

In the past, particularly in poorer countries, it was difficult enough for parents to find the money to send their children to primary school. Middle school and upper school were even more difficult. So often poor families who wanted their children to get more education would encourage them to go into a seminary. The seminaries would accept the boys even if they said: "I'm not sure if I have a vocation, but who knows? I am willing, and I *think* I'd like to be a priest." But in the end what happened was, out of a class of thirty or forty boys only two or three would actually become priests.

Shortage of Vocations?

As far as Brazil is concerned, I think it's important to point out that the period when most young men wanted to become priests was also a time of extreme clericalism: when everything in the church had to be done by priests. Of course the laity were necessary as well: lay people had to be there at Mass, to say the prayers. And sometimes the clergy asked for their help, in organizing processions or collecting money. They were very good and useful at that. Sometimes certain priests even went so far as to discuss religious matters with the laity and ask their opinions. But final decisions were always made by the clergy, usually by the bishops.

And since priests had to do everything, decide everything, take every responsibility and since there was no question of the laity sharing their work, or their confidence, it was not surprising that there were so many priests. We needed them. And in order to do anything in the church, you had to be a priest.

Today it's different. Now the clergy really rely on the laity and respect their rightful place in the church of Christ — which is very different from granting them this place as a favor. It's extraordinary how the church has progressed and evolved. Step by step. Take the Catholic Action movement, for instance: that represented an enormous leap forward. It achieved a great deal; but it was still only a beginning. It merely conceded to the laity the honor of participating in the hierarchical ministry of the church. The apostle was the bishop. The apostle's immediate collaborator was the priest. But certain members of the laity were allowed to participate in the apostolate of the bishops and priests. It was a great honor. There was even some discussion about whether they should be granted the right to "participate" or to "collaborate"! It was a very important question! Nowadays we've got beyond all of that. We are very grateful to Catholic Action because it did the pioneering work and blazed the trail.

Without it, the Second Vatican Council would probably have been a great deal less effective. But today we really respect the apostolic role of the laity in practice, not just in theory.

On the whole there aren't any more boarding seminaries. The pupils live together in small communities. Often they work as well. Usually today you can't enter a seminary until you have finished your secondary education. So you'd be sixteen or seventeen. These small groups of candidates for the priesthood maintain close contact with a priest, who supervises their progress. And they attend courses at a theological college.

They do more than just philosophy and theology at a theological college these days. In my day, when we graduated from the seminary we were rather proud of ourselves. First of all we had studied the Greek and Latin humanities, and that made us particularly proud. We were convinced that just studying the language and literature of Greece and Rome could develop the mind! Afterward we did philosophy, and after that, theology. We were utterly convinced that all of this made us rather superior, even compared to other young people of our own age who had studied at the best schools and universities: whether they had studied law, medicine, literature, even philosophy, nothing matched a seminary education!

Imagine our immense surprise, when upon leaving the seminary we encountered young economists, young sociologists, when we found ourselves in a world where science and technology were just beginning to develop. It was a shock, but a providential shock: it made us realize that something had to be changed.

There was something else as well. We were very ill-prepared for pastoral work, for serving the people. On Sundays we went to give catechism classes to poor children. Normally they were very young children. It was exceptional to have an adolescent in the class. There was no question of our living among the people, or even finding out about real human problems. And so afterward we didn't even know how to talk about them. Our language was all wrong. When we preached our sermons were so sophisticated, grounded as they were in Greek and Latin literature, scholastic philosophy, and Thomistic theology, that they went right over the heads of our congregations.

We bore the stamp of the Counter-Reformation. We in the church lost a great deal of time because we were so preoccupied with defending ourselves. We were very good at justifying our religion, but it was above all a defensive justification. It's true, we knew how to refute errors. My God! We knew every heresy by heart! We tracked them down, century by century; and we were always on the lookout for new ones. In my seminary there was a whole campaign against modernism.

But what I want to emphasize is that when the Spirit of the Lord filled us with the need to come closer to the people, we realized that we were strangers to them. All of us. Strangers to the people, especially to the simplest, the humblest, the poorest people. We had to learn their language. And not just their language: their way of thinking, too. We came out of seminary with our heads full of logic. We were Cartesians. We thought in premises and conclusions. We were dealers in syllogisms, purely and simply. And that isn't how people think. The discovery of reality shocked us all.

When I left the seminary I had only one idea about social matters, and it was quite simple. I had the impression that the world was increasingly divided into two opposing camps: capitalism and communism. Communism was evil, the evil of evils; it was intrinsically perverse.

It took me some time to discover that a system like capitalism, which puts profit before people, is also intrinsically evil. ... It is capitalism that is intrinsically evil. Even today, when it's no longer possible to talk of capitalism in the singular, because there are several different forms of it, profit remains the primary concern.   — CB, 41–48

BASE COMMUNITIES AND THE LAITY

At one time I believed that institutions could be converted: I mean universities, trade unions, big organizations, the press....

But that was an impossible dream. Today I realize that the ways of the Lord are not exactly our ways. My hope lies now in the grassroots communities.

Think of a parish priest. He's probably quite happy because he has six, seven, eight Masses on a Sunday and his church is full every time. But you know very well that the people who come to Mass, particularly in the cities — even in Rome! — represent only a small percentage of the population. And what about the others? All the people who don't come to church? They're living their own lives in their own neighborhoods, their own natural communities. So now we've begun to approach these communities. Nuns and priests, and above all lay workers, are trying to live and work among them, are trying to help people to identify their problems and organize themselves to solve them. We say to these men and women who wish to work for human advancement: "Don't think that the government is going to come here and solve your problems for you! You've got to think for yourselves, act for yourselves. Later perhaps, when the government sees you all united, it may come and help." And it's the same with the church. We can't expect everything to be thought of and arranged and decided from without, by the powers that be, on behalf of everyone. We must imitate Christ. Christ came for everybody, for all people of all countries and all times. But nevertheless he became incarnate among one race, in one society. He adopted a language and customs that were not the language and customs of all people of all countries and all times. He was the son of a Nazareth carpenter. We need to understand this lesson of incarnation: we must each remain bound to humanity as a whole, and to the universal church, but at the same time become incarnate in our own particular Nazareth.

I think it's really impossible now to bring about changes from the top. The real changes will come from below.... The grassroots communities are revealing new possibilities and teaching us new lessons....

For example, for a long time we had a rather ill-considered, negative attitude toward what we called "popular religiosity."

We saw it as being riddled with superstition, even magic. Consequently it was considered a vital objective of pastoral work to abolish all traditional processions and ceremonies. But today we are beginning to understand the words of Christ: "I thank Thee, O Father, because Thou hast hidden thy truths from the great and the wise and the powerful, and Thou hast revealed them to the humble." Now we have the people's evangelical movement known as the Brothers' Meeting. There are some people in the groups who are educated, who have been to university; but many more who are illiterate, or semi-literate. Someone reads an extract from the Gospel, and then they all talk about it. And it's extraordinary how often the most profound, the most relevant comments come from the poorest and simplest people.

— CB, 120–22

LISTENING TO THE PEOPLE

I think the word "prophet" is used in an overspecialized sense, as though the Lord charged only a small number of people with the responsibility of being one. But all of us as members of the church have a prophetic mission. The whole church is called to be prophetic, that is to say, to proclaim the word of the Lord and also to lend the Lord's voice to those who have no voice, to do exactly what Christ, when reading from Isaiah, declared his own personal mission to be: "The spirit of the Lord is on me. He has sent me to bring the good news to the poor, to open their eyes and set them free." This has always been the church's mission.

As with prophecy, I always say, so with holiness: although admittedly, in the words of the hymn, "the Lord alone is holy," essentially holy. But by baptism, by sanctifying grace, we are made sharers in the Lord's holiness. This isn't a favor reserved for the few. It's a gift and an obligation for us all. And being holy doesn't mean having visions or working miracles. It means living by sanctifying grace, constantly mindful that we carry Christ within us and that we walk within God.

— TTG, 43–44

A CRISIS OF AUTHORITY?

You know, if you look at the history of the church, you find that every great Council has been followed by a crisis. There are always some people who hang on to the past and make it their duty to defend the true church. They exaggerate. And there are always others who exaggerate in the opposite direction. Balance is something that we find very difficult. It isn't surprising: the Creator brought together several different worlds in one creature. We are brothers to stones, trees, animals, angels, and God himself. And these different worlds cause conflict and struggle within each of us.

Attitudes and structures were so profoundly shaken by the Council that it would have been inconceivable for everything to go smoothly, quietly, and harmoniously afterward. It would have been disturbing if there hadn't been collisions and clashes and conflicts: it would have meant that the Council had said nothing and done nothing.

As far as I am concerned the backwash of the period after the Council is not the real problem. The real problem, I repeat, is our lack of courage when it comes to putting the conclusions of the Council into practice — or, for us Latin Americans, the conclusions of Medellín: in other words, putting into practice the Gospel as we bishops, with the pope and under the guidance of the Holy Spirit, have interpreted it for the people and the world of today.

I know that many people talk about a crisis of authority in the church, and even a crisis of faith. My personal experience has taught me that a crisis of authority is most likely to come about when the authorities haven't the courage to accept the consequences of the resolutions they have studied, discussed, voted for and ratified. If there is a crisis of authority it may also be because we who are in authority forget that exercising authority means serving, and not being served. Authoritarian authority is impossible nowadays: authority can stem only from dialogue and mutual fraternal consideration.   — *CB*, 169–70

LIBERATION THEOLOGY

When you look at our continent, where more than two-thirds of the people live in subhuman conditions as a result of injustices, and when you see that the same situation is repeated all over the world, how can you help wanting to work toward human liberation? Just as the Father, the Creator, wants us to be co-creators, so the Son, the Redeemer, wants us to be co-redeemers. So it is up to us to continue the work of liberation begun by the Son: the liberation from sin and the consequences of sin, the liberation from egoism and the consequences of egoism. That is what the theology of liberation means to us, and I see no reason why anyone should be afraid of a true, authentic theology of liberation.   — CB, 170–71

The people already understand that we have no right to blame God for the problems that we have created ourselves. As if the Lord were responsible for the floods or the droughts! No! It would have been very easy for our Father to create a universe that was already perfect. But it would have been terribly boring for us to come into a world where everything had already been done, and done well, where everything was complete. So the Lord merely began the creative process and entrusted man with the task of completing it. It is up to us to control the rivers. It's a question of intelligence and integrity. If we had shown sufficient intelligence and integrity in the past the droughts and the floods would already have been controlled. Nowadays deserts are being watered and rivers diverted. It's our own problem, not the Lord's....

For a long time we preached a very passive sort of religion: "We must all have patience, be obedient, resign ourselves. We must accept suffering in this life in union with the suffering of Christ." And a religion that called on magic. If there was a drought, we would organize a procession to pray for rain. And if too much rain fell, we'd have another procession....

We must be thankful that with the Lord's help we are beginning to change people's way of thinking and change their attitudes. But you have to start from where the people are. If I were to begin by abolishing all processions — or if I decided, for example, not to baptize children any longer because I can't evangelize them — I wouldn't get very far. It has to be a gradual process, this helping the people forward.   — *CB, 124–26*

THE VOICE OF THE VOICELESS WORLD

I would like to summarize my deepest social convictions, which have matured over the years:

- I do not desire a hostile confrontation between the rich world and the poor world.

- I believe in the violence of the peacemakers, in the moral pressure that liberates man.

- I cannot believe that the universe, created through love, will end in hatred.

I would like to say to everyone:

- Where man is, the church must be present.

- The egoism of the rich presents a more serious problem than Communism.

- Today's world is threatened by the atom bomb of squalid poverty.

- Profound changes must be made in order to establish justice in every sphere throughout the world.

- Without a deep personal conversion, no one can become an instrument for the conversion of the world.

- The social revolution will not be achieved in the developing countries unless there is a parallel moral and social revolution in the developed countries.

- We have to build on solid ground. It is not enough to conduct literacy campaigns for the masses. The work, the real work, consists in awakening consciences so that the masses may eventually become a people.

- To revolutionize the world, the only thing needed is for us to live and to spread the Gospel of Jesus Christ with real conviction.

- Dire poverty is revolting and degrading; it taints the image of God in every man.

- We have no right to blame God for injustice and its attendant evils; it is for us to do away with injustice.

- My door and my heart are open to all — to all without exception.

- Christ has prophesied what will happen at the last judgment: we shall be judged according to the way we have treated him in the persons of the poor, the oppressed, the downtrodden.

Let me now turn to God and translate in my prayer the hope of those who are voiceless in a world that crushes them:

> Father,
> how can we fail
> to gather all mankind
> into prayer,
> since your Divine Son,
> our brother,
> Jesus Christ,
> shed his blood
> for all men,
> of all lands,
> of all times?
>
> But hear, O Lord,
> my special prayer
> for my people,
> the voiceless ones.

There are thousands
and thousands
of human creatures
in the poor countries,
and in the slums
of the rich countries,
with no right
to raise their voices,
no possibility
of claiming
of protesting,
however just
are the rights
they have to uphold.

The homeless,
the starving,
the ragged,
the wasted,
with no chance
of education,
no work,
no future,
no hope;
they may end up
believing
it was meant to be,
and losing heart,
become the silent,
the voiceless ones.

If all of us
who believe in You
had helped our rich brothers,
by opening their eyes,
stirring their consciences,
the unjust
would not have advanced,

and the gap
between rich and poor,
between individuals and groups,
between countries,
even between continents,
would not be so glaring.

Do in us, O Lord,
what we have failed
and still fail to do.
How difficult it is
to get beyond the barrier
of aid, of gifts,
of assistance,
and reach the
realm of justice!
The privileged grow angry:
our judgment
is unfair, they say.
Meanwhile they discover subversion
and Communism
in the most democratic,
the most human, the most
Christian gestures!
Amen.   — *CRSA*, 46–60

2

From Paternalism to Liberation

*Dom Helder was a passionate man, a gifted communicator, net-
worker, and organizer. As a student and a young priest, a very
young priest, in the conservative church climate of the time, he
found his home in the Brazilian version of fascism, engaging in
adolescent polemics, rabble-rousing, and even violence. In his
thirties and forties, in Rio de Janeiro, he devoted his energy
to improving Catholic education, to preaching and lecturing,
and subsequently to organizing Catholic Action. He proved a
successful organizer of major events, culminating in the International Eucharistic Congress held in Rio de Janeiro in 1955.
We have heard his story of how the archbishop of Lyon, France,
challenged him to use these talents in the service of the poor.
With typical self-mockery, Dom Helder described how his housing program and his Providence Bank were inadequate to cope
with the flood of immigrants from Brazil's rural areas to the
cities. He began to think about the causes of poverty, what he
later came to call "structures of injustice." "Structural sin" was
a concept in vogue in Latin American liberation theology.*

*Dom Helder had already been involved in politics, but more
as a political operator, knowing which levers to pull, which
shoulders to pat, to get advantages for the church, or even jobs
for friends. Now he began to have a deeper concept of politics.
This concept was widened still further when he was involved
with the debates provoked by the Second Vatican Council, particularly Father Louis Lebret's ideas on world development,*

which helped to shape Pope Paul VI's encyclical Populorum Progressio.

This intellectual and ideological development is the subject of this chapter. Back in Brazil, he sought to harness the energy of the church to promote development and consulted the experts of the United Nations Commission for Latin America, CEPAL, to refine his ideas. He became a friend of the Brazilian developmental economist Celso Furtado. He was enthused by the developmental ideas of President Juscelino Kubitschek, who built the futuristic new capital, Brasília, to open up the unoccupied center and north of the country and set up a regional development agency for the North-East, SUDENE, of which Dom Helder was a firm supporter. In the environment of the 1970s, it is not surprising that he should declare himself a socialist, though never a communist. Dom Helder came to believe firmly that no political or social programs could succeed without the active participation of ordinary people. He launched a movement, Moral Pressure for Liberation, to work, by nonviolent means, for a "social revolution." His vision of the movement was inspired by the example of Dr. Martin Luther King and also by Gandhi, and one of these movements was to be launched on the hundredth anniversary of Gandhi's birth, October 2, 1968. For the launch of the movement Dom Helder secured the signatures of nineteen Latin American bishops from CELAM and forty-three Brazilian bishops. He discussed the idea with other participants in the Latin American bishops' conference in Medellín, Colombia, where he helped to draft the eloquent declaration of the church's commitment to justice. Because some people were worried that the name would be confused with Moral Rearmament, he relaunched it in October as Action, Justice, and Peace.

While never wavering in his loyalty to the pope and in his fidelity to traditional Catholic practice, Dom Helder began to believe that institutions alone would never bring lasting progress, and that what had to be done was to inspire and nurture minorities within all institutions, all cultures, all religions. He argued that all who worked to benefit their fellow human beings were inspired by the God he knew from the Jewish and Christian scriptures, by the Holy Spirit. This is the origin of his idea of "Abrahamic minorities." The most eloquent expression of this idea is in the book The Desert Is Fertile, *extracts from which end this chapter.*

THE CHURCH AND DEVELOPMENT

The text that follows is part of an address prepared for the Tenth Extraordinary Assembly of the Latin American Episcopal Council which took place at Mar del Plata (near Buenos Aires, Argentina) from October 9 to October 16, 1966, on the theme: "The active presence of the church in the development and integration of Latin America, in the light of the principles of the second Vatican Council."

This text is perhaps the most developed treatment of Dom Helder's views on the role of the church in addressing the challenge of poverty. It shows him with a coherent theory of development and underdevelopment. Characteristic features are the stress on the social impact of the church on the Latin American continent, notably its acceptance of the social system, including slavery, as something that cannot be isolated from its "spiritual" role, and awareness of the political nature of development, notably in the concept of "internal colonialism." There is another challenge to what Dom Helder sees as a false spiritualization of the church's role when he remarks that Latin America's "number one problem" is not the shortage of vocations to the priesthood, but underdevelopment. This text, written over forty years ago, identifies issues that are still crucial for world development today, food security, protectionism, economic integration. Even where an issue, such as Marxism or communism, seems to belong to the past, equivalent threats, equally a mixture of fact and propaganda, are not wanting today: security, terrorism, and subversion are examples.

Development Is Human Realization

Human alienation can result either from ignoring time in favor of eternity, or from ignoring eternity in favor of time. They are the two faces of alienation.

Marx would never have presented religion as the opium of the people and the church as alienated and alienating if he had seen around him a church made flesh, continuing the incarnation of Christ; if he had seen Christians who really and practically loved men as the primary expression of their love for God; if he had seen the days of Vatican II, which sums up what theology can say about terrestrial reality.

It is clear that the transcendental side of man is as real as the economic. And moreover, we must remember a historic event of outstanding importance, now that man, who in twenty years has lived twenty thousand, is but a step from considering himself God: God himself was made man, to accomplish the divinization of all people. Development therefore is the realization of man in his full human dimension and, by the grace of God, in his divine dimension.

No country and no people can develop alone. The world has become interdependent. The presence of the church in the development of Latin America will be meaningful and effectual only insofar as it forms part of a total effort at presence in the world.

Social Revolution and Conversion

Who has no need of conversion, even several conversions? We are all of us in need of continual conversion. And nations, which are assemblies of individuals, are all of them, without exception, in need of continual conversion. There are not innocent people and sinful people. The only difference lies in the concentration of faults, all of which arise — as in the case of individuals — from self-centeredness.

The social revolution that the world needs will not come by act of parliament, nor by guerilla warfare, or by war. It is a profound and radical transformation that presupposes divine grace, a movement of world opinion that can and must be helped and stimulated by the church of Latin America and of the whole world.

The Responsibility of the Latin American Church

Latin American society, since its discovery, has grown and developed under the influence of the church. All its structures, social, economic, political, and cultural, have undergone the influence of Iberian Christianity. The struggles for independence brought about little change in these structures. Today, for the first time, we are witnessing the dawn of a substantial transformation. The church is indissolubly bound to this history, with its values, its authentic triumphs and moments of greatness, but also with its errors, its dissonances and aberrations.

Today, because of this, the church is faced with unquestionable responsibility and inescapable obligations. The church herself contributed to the authentic values of our civilization and cannot permit them to be crushed by the strident advance of urgent and inevitable structural changes. But the church is also called to denounce collective sin, unjust and rigid structures, not simply as one who judges from without but as one who acknowledges her own share of the responsibility and of the blame. The church must be aware of her part in this history, and thus play her part with greater solidarity in the present and in the future.

Whatever the course of history, the fact is that the church today finds herself effectively present in a developing Latin America. This human situation of crisis in society demands a self-awakening on the part of the church and a decisive effort to help the continent to achieve its liberation from underdevelopment. If this mission is to be fulfilled, the church must undergo a radical purification and conversion. Her relationships with the underdeveloped masses, with diverse groups and with all types of organization, must become more and more relationships of service. Her strength must be calculated less in terms of prestige and power and more in terms of the Gospel and of service to men. In this way, she will be in a position to reveal to the people of this anguished continent the true face of Christ.

Purpose of the Church's Presence

To help in the conversion of the continent. If Latin America desires the conversion of others, and especially of the developed world, it must sincerely and decisively begin by converting itself. It would have no moral force to speak to others if it lacked the courage to face up to its own defects as a people and to do every-thing possible to overcome them. Spiritual leaders, and Christian leaders in particular, have an important role in this conversion, above all because the impetus to reform must come from them.

To stimulate in Latin America an awareness of its task in the world. No one is in the world by chance. There is no such thing as chance, only divine providence. From all eternity, the hum-blest of men is present to the will of the Father and must fulfill his mission, whether it is great or small. What is important is that he should not opt out of the plan of love that regards men not as objects, but as subjects and co-creators.

If these remarks are valid for the individual, there is no reason why they should not hold for the nation. It was not by chance that Christopher Columbus landed in America. It was not by chance that our various peoples won their victories and suffered their defeats. And it is not by chance that we have our hopes and our disappointments. What is expected of us by the Father?

What must we do to conform to the plan of God? What is required of us that we be abreast of the times in which we are living?

Internal Colonialism

It is probably not far wrong to say that the collective sin of Latin America, the synthesis of our sins as a people, is inter-nal colonialism. This expression can give rise to equivocation and cause ill feeling if it is not clearly explained. By "internal colonialism," we mean the relationship of some developed regions with other underdeveloped regions in the same country (for example, the Brazilian industry of the South-Central has made large profits from the flow of raw materials supplied by the North-East and the North, both of which are still underdeveloped).

"Internal colonialism" means that a great part of rural Latin America continues to live in the Middle Ages. We need to find ways of expressing this that do not cause injury or, at least, that manifest love and concern in the manner of a surgeon who operates to save and to cure. Hiding the truth is not friendship. Nor is it friendship to proclaim the truth in a loveless manner. If one of the signs of our age is the ending of colonialism (at least open political colonialism), how can we permit people to treat their fellow countrymen in the way Europeans once treated Africans? We know that there are exceptions and are grateful for this. We have no wish to ignore the complexity of the situation and the circumstances that lead to blindness and to the apparent insensitivity that tolerates subhuman conditions of housing, clothing, food, education, and work among the rural populations of our underdeveloped areas....

The Effect of Defending Privileges

Fear of a Self-Awakening. It is easy to say that Latin America is the Catholic continent, the reserve of Christianity for the whole world. But the Latin American masses will open their eyes, with us or without us or against us. There are no longer towering walls to separate peoples from one another. The means of communication overcome any effort at isolation. And woe to Christianity when the eyes of the people are opened if the masses have the impression that they were abandoned on account of the church's connivance with the rich and the powerful.

But apart from the risk of losing prestige in the eyes of the people — the problem is not one of prestige but of a mission to serve — it is our task, our human and Christian duty to help the children of God to emerge from the subhuman situation in which they now exist. Destitution degrades the human person and is an affront to the Creator and Father.

At this point we are advised to be prudent: it is easier and quicker (it is said) to open the eyes of the masses, to rouse them to consciousness, to make them aware of their situation, than it is to bring about structural reform. And if anyone, knowing this, promotes a self-awakening among the people — the pessimists say — he is playing with subversion, playing with communism, setting one class against the other.

It is striking to discover the extremes to which we are led by the defense of privileges. Concern with Marxism would preserve religion as the opium of the people and the church as an alienating force. How can we ignore the beauty and the strength, the democracy and the Christian potential of the endeavor to awaken the masses? It is a question of putting the creature on his feet, of arousing his sense of initiative, of working in groups, of a sense of responsibility; it is a question of altering the attitude that waits for the government to do everything.

Poverty that is transmitted from father to son, from grandfather to grandson, leaves marks that it is difficult to eradicate: the man who depends on others for everything, who is an outcast, an object of assistance and paternalism and not a subject of rights and justice; the man who is at the mercy of the good or ill will of an almighty boss (for whom there are no laws, no authority, no justice, and on whose judgment all depends) ends by acquiring the mentality of a slave. How can he avoid falling into fatalism and confusing dangerously the religion of his employer with the superstition and magic of the slaves? How can he avoid resigning himself to his fate, desperation, dejection today and rebellion tomorrow? The rudiments of education are not sufficient for cases like these, even if they are complemented by the fiction of voting rights. We have no wish to ignore the complexity of the consequences of self-awakening, and we shall make some concrete suggestions in this regard. But for the present, let us admit a fear of such a self-awakening, which is in practice a conscious or unconscious defense of privileges.

Distortion of Christian Principles

The Christian principles invoked in defense of order are numer-ous — as if the concrete situation in our areas deserved the name of order. Absurd privileges are upheld in the name of the princi-ple of property. The dignity of the human person is invoked as if the dignity of the workers were non-existent. Liberty is threat-ened and must be defended, but little is said about a liberty that has been crushed for centuries.   — CC, 112–20

DEVELOPMENT IS NOT LIBERATION

[Brazilian President Juscelino] Kubitschek was the man who threw out the incredible, spectacular challenge: "Fifty years in five!" Five years is the presidential term of office. Fifty years was how far Brazil lagged behind the developed world. Kubitschek conceived of a nationwide development plan: he assembled a team of experts, and he put the plan into operation.

But Kubitschek and all his experts, and all of us in the church, were extremely naive: we weren't aware, for instance, of the power of the multinationals. We weren't aware of the alliance that already existed between the huge multinational corpora-tions that were offering us aid and the privileged classes inside Brazil. Without wanting to we merely added to the burden of oppression, reinforced the unjust structures under which the people suffered. That's why we must think now about liberation and help to bring about the liberation of the people. — CB, 91

BUT THERE WILL ALWAYS BE
A NEED FOR CHARITY

Ever the realist, Dom Helder was aware that grand transforma-tions of structures do not do away with the need for charity. He made this point in an anecdote about a meeting with U.S. arch-bishop Fulton Sheen, a prominent TV personality of the 1950s.

He was auxiliary bishop of New York. He had become a television personality, and he came to Rio de Janeiro for three days
when he was at the height of his fame. I stayed with him all the
time he was here; I went everywhere with him. We were very
close friends.

On the last day, just before he was leaving, I said to him: "Do
you mind if I ask you something? After spending these three
days with you I know that we have a great deal in common,
we share the same attitudes toward the world and the church.
Why don't you take advantage of your reputation, and of television, which can work miracles, and campaign against, say,
racism? Why don't you make use of the power you have at your
disposal and denounce, for example, the injustices of the international politics of commerce? Why do you associate yourself
with attitudes that neither of us agrees with?"

And he answered: "My brother, I am glad that you had the
courage and the confidence in me to ask that question. You
might have gone on wondering without saying anything to me.
But I can explain it very simply. As you know the bishops of the
United States donate 1 million dollars a year to Latin America.
Thanks to television, I'm also able to raise 80 million dollars a
year for the Holy Father's Propaganda Fide. This money enables
the pope to help schools, leper hospitals, and general hospitals
all over the world. Now I assure you that if I were to go on
television tomorrow and denounce racism or the injustice of the
international politics of commerce, this money would immédi-
ately stop coming in. So it is a choice that I have had to make.
I prefer to be considered weak or naive or unprincipled. I'm
quite aware that that is how I appear; and I accept it. Someone has to sacrifice himself for the sake of the emergency work,
while others work toward structural change. I am glad that my
brother Dom Helder speaks the truths that I am not able to
speak. In a way, you see, we are complementary."

After that I kissed his hands. I was very moved: "So you
accept.... That is true poverty, to accept being judged naive,
bourgeois, blind to injustice. And you have chosen it deliberately." I kissed his hands.

When you are working for human advancement you discover that there are — and no doubt always will be — some people who cannot really benefit from that advancement. Something — whether it's old age, ill health, or the consequences of malnutrition — holds them back and leaves them by the wayside. Perhaps I could draw a military analogy — although as you know I hate war! An army decides to capture a town and marches toward it. The troops must not forget for one moment that their objective is to defeat and take possession of the town. But if along the way they come across people who are wounded and can't fight, and who may die if they are not cared for; and if the troops can help them, carry them on their shoulders, or take them to a hospital, without losing sight of their own objective — then they must do it. I often think that in the war against injustice 80 percent of our time and efforts must be devoted to changing structures and promoting human advancement; but 20 percent must be set aside for tending the wounded and the victims of the war. — *CB*, 137–38

MORAL PRESSURE FOR LIBERATION

A threefold mutation of mentalities (cultural revolution in a new sense) is a fundamental necessity in our case, as preliminary to the profound and rapid changes we want to achieve.

It is urgently necessary to sensitize the powerful so they will of themselves decide to give up their privileges, and also to sensitize Latin American governments so they will decide to bring about basic reforms.

It is urgently necessary that young people try to discover adequate solutions to our real problems.

It is urgently necessary that we aid the masses to become a people. — *VP*, 58

That's the argument military men always use when trying to convince me that I'm a subversive and a Communist. They tell me, "You, personally, are a good man. But it's easier and quicker to arouse the consciousness of the masses, to open their eyes, much easier than to carry out reforms. If you go on waking up the masses," they say, "then you are preparing the revolution! You are a subversive. You are playing the game of the Communists!" To this I make my reply. "You are under a delusion," I tell them. "You think that if the church refrains from opening the eyes of the masses, the eyes of the masses will remain shut. But they will not. Whether with us or against us, their eyes will be opened." And when occasionally someone tells us that the church is moving too quickly, my opinion is that we are four centuries behind. We accepted African slavery. Oh, I know: the epoch wanted and condoned slavery and I don't believe I am either more clairvoyant or devout or Christian than my forebears were. No doubt, had I myself lived in that period I would have accepted the institution of slavery. I might even have owned slaves; it was done in that era. But the plain truth is that we did accept the slavery of Africans for three whole centuries.

Well, I ask you: what could a priest say at Mass in "the big house," confronting the Savior and confronting the slaves? He preached patience, the acceptance of suffering along with the suffering of Christ. I know that these are great virtues. We will always need patience, and it will always be very important to offer our sufferings in union with Christ's suffering. But within that framework, the church played the game of the oppressors.

After the abolition of black slavery, we continued and still continue to accept the enslaving of the native-born. That is why we must carry out this work of waking up the masses, even though we are aware of the risks.   — *VP*, 74

THE LIMITATIONS OF VIOLENCE

Allow me the humble courage of taking a stand: I respect those who have felt obliged in conscience to opt for violence, not the facile violence of armchair-guerillas, but that of the men who have proved their sincerity by the sacrifice of their lives. It seems to me that the memory of Camilo Torres and Che Guevara deserves as much respect as that of Dr. Martin Luther King. I accuse the real abettors of violence, all those on the right or on the left who wrong justice and prevent peace.

My personal vocation is to be a pilgrim of peace, following the example of Paul VI. Personally I would prefer a thousand times more to be killed than to kill anyone.

This personal position is founded on the Gospel.... We need only to turn to the Beatitudes — the quintessence of the Gospel message — to see that the option for Christians is clear. We, as Christians, are on the side of nonviolence, and this is in no way an option for weakness and passivity. Opting for nonviolence means to believe more strongly in the power of truth, justice, and love than in the power of wars, weapons, and hatred.

— *VP,* 57

Let me tell you why I have no faith in violence. I have two reasons. As I constantly repeat, I am quite aware that already, in Latin America, violence is established. Because, if a quite small minority exists whose wealth is based on the misery of a great number, that is already violence. But if we caused a war of liberation to explode, it would immediately be crushed by the imperialistic powers. Powers, in the plural. The United States cannot accept a second Cuba in Latin America, its sphere of influence. And Soviet Russia would obviously come immediately. And Red China and Cuba.

Ever since the small attempts at revolution in Bolivia and Colombia, there are military bases everywhere in Latin America, capable of crushing every sort of guerilla warfare. The strength of the guerilla fighters was in training their men in regions where modern armaments are completely meaningless. But today, at the anti-guerilla bases, soldiers are being trained precisely for those infernos, those inaccessible regions. I was in Colombia and I saw, in regions that were formerly the domain of the guerrilleros, an anti-guerilla base where, for example, the soldiers let themselves be bitten by snakes in order to be vaccinated and prepared for no matter what test.

That is my first reason. I have no interest at all in causing a war to break out, even a war of liberation, if I am convinced that it would be immediately crushed.

And I have another reason. The revolution will not be fought either by the students or the priests or the artists or the intellectuals; it will be fought by the masses, the oppressed, and they will be the victims of that repressive action of the powers.

I am in direct contact with the masses, and I know that underdevelopment, both physical and material, unfortunately carries with it a spiritual underdevelopment. There is a discouragement, a lack of reasons for living, a fatalism. Why die? Very often in Latin America the masses have risen in revolt only to die and cause others to die. But they know all too well that the great of the world may change among themselves, but as for the oppressed, they always remain sunk in misery. They have no real reasons to live.

It seems to me that in the next ten or fifteen years there will really be no possibility of mobilizing the masses for a war of liberation.

I respect and shall always respect those who, with a clear conscience, have chosen or choose or will choose violence. I do not respect the drawing room guerrilleros, but the real ones. Yes, I respect them. But since they recognize that there are no real chances for violence in the next ten or fifteen years, I tell them "Then give me that time. I am going to do an experiment."

I think Camilo Torres was one of many young priests and laymen who lost faith, not in Christ, but in the institutional church, when they saw all the fine resolutions of the Vatican Council trapped by human weakness and ecclesiastical prudence. Like others, Camilo Torres believed that the only way he could really help to liberate his people was through guerilla warfare, and he chose to join a Communist underground group. I also think that the Colombian Communists took advantage of Torres's reputation and deliberately sent him on a mission where he was likely to be killed. For them the end justified the means. The end was to make known and to popularize the existence of the guerilla movement. The means was to have a celebrated martyr.

Camilo Torres died, and neither the young people nor the workers of Colombia came forward to help the guerillas. Our Colombian brethren were very frustrated.

But you see it was like Che Guevara's failure in Bolivia. Che Guevara had a natural genius for guerilla warfare, and he had seen its effects in Cuba. But his mistake was to forget that a mass of people is not the same as a united people. A mass only becomes a united people after a long and difficult campaign during which the people are gradually and quietly made more aware. The majority of Bolivians, like nearly all Latin Americans, were living in subhuman conditions; but since they had no reason for living they also had no reason for dying. The Bolivian peasants welcomed Che Guevara and his men because they were armed. But afterward, when the government soldiers came, they welcomed them as well and told them everything they knew about the guerillas and their hiding places.

All of this only made me more and more certain that liberation could never be achieved through armed struggle.

— CB, 176–77

CAPITALISM AND SOCIALISM

The United States is a living demonstration of the internal contradictions in the capitalist regime. It manages to create underdeveloped strata in the very heart of the richest country in the world. There are 30 million inhabitants of that richest country who are living in conditions unworthy of human beings. The U.S.A. manages to arouse fratricidal conflicts between the whites and blacks; with the pretext of anticommunism, but in fact out of a thirst for prestige and expansion of its sphere of influence, it conducts the most shameful war the world has ever known. The dominant system in the United States is so irrational that it seems to be creating a one-dimensional robot existence that leads the young of various cultural traditions to feel impelled to construct a more just and more humane society, a new social context for humanizing technology.

— *VP*, 87–88

I am thinking of a conscious and deliberate participation by more classes of the population in the control of power and the sharing of wealth and culture. I am thinking of a future when people will become the agents of their social progress; when the whole of society will attain a high level of science and professional aptitude; when humanity will be free, when man will be the protagonist of a society for which he will constantly be more responsible on every plane — local, regional, national, continental, worldwide; of a society in which the state as subsidiary authority will respect the responsibility of each individual and his entire participation in the life of that society; of a government in which the state will respect minorities and favor without any discrimination a better harmony among ethnic, ideological, and religious groups; of a state where the structures tend toward an ever wider socialization, in which exist and function basic organizations and intermediary and independent institutions that are responsible and organized. I believe that mankind can arrive at a rational and functional and planned society and, in international affairs, a self-determination of the nations and a balanced integration....

Why not recognize that there is no such thing as a unique type of socialism? Why not demand, for the Christian, the free use of the word "socialism"? It is not necessarily linked with materialism, nor does it have to designate a system that destroys the individual or the community. It can designate a regime that is at the service of the community and the individual.

— *VP*, 89–90

FROM DEVELOPMENT TO LIBERATION

Personally, ... I became very involved in the idea of "development." The word conveyed a hope for solidarity and for real collaboration between rich and poor countries. The increasing gap between the minority of rich countries and the majority of poor countries might be bridged. But it very soon became evident that the developed countries' resolution to set aside 1 percent of their gross national product for aid to underdeveloped countries was not going to solve the problem. And that the problem would also not be solved by raising this figure to 2, 3, or even 4 percent. Paul VI was courageous enough to say that what the developed countries gave with one hand they took away with the other.

When I speak of aid from developed countries I always distinguish between private and official aid. I am always grateful for any disinterested help from our richer brethren. While we are fighting to secure justice, this help enables us to rescue the victims of injustice and save them from a miserable death. But I am very fearful of official aid, which eases the donor's conscience and gives the impression that everything that can be done is being done, while the heart of the problem is forgotten. And the heart of the problem, of course, is the unjust politics of international commerce. At the end of the first "decade for development," President Nixon himself was forced to admit that the rich countries were emerging from the decade richer and the poor countries poorer.   — *CB*, 172–73

"I DISCOVERED MINORITIES"

I was forced to accept that institutions as a whole are too cumbersome.... It isn't easy to mobilize even a single university: it's impossible to mobilize several. And it's the same with churches, and trade unions....

So then I discovered minorities. It's true that all the various institutions taken as a whole are difficult to move; but it's also absolutely true, experimentally demonstrable, that in every institution, every human group everywhere, no matter what the country, race, or religion, there are minorities who, beneath a vast diversity of denominations, leaders, and objectives, share a common hunger and thirst for justice: minorities for whom justice is the path of peace. I call them "Abrahamic minorities" in honor of Abraham, the father of all those who over the centuries have continued to hope against hope. But I should like to find a more universal name for them: Jews and Moslems and Christians know Abraham, but Abraham means nothing in the East. I now believe that the moral pressure to liberate mankind will come not from institutions as a whole, but from the minorities that I still call Abrahamic....

At one point our friends in Holland made an attempt to bring together the leaders of active non-violent movements all over the world. They wanted me to lend my name to the meeting and be, if you like, the leader of leaders. But I refused.

It isn't a leader that we lack. The action of one man, or even one organization, will not make the minorities strong. The Holy Spirit has inspired all of these different groups throughout the world, and only the Holy Spirit can make them effective. The vast audiences that I find wherever I am invited to speak are united by a common desire: not to see a particular man, or hear a pop singer, or join an organization, or adopt a slogan. What they share is the same hunger and thirst for justice as the path to peace....

When God undertakes a task he wants men to collaborate with him; but he helps us, he doesn't abandon us. What we lack is a way of creating links between the minorities, and of uniting them — without unifying them — in common aims. It will come! And I am sure that the solution, the method, will come from young people. We have already seen some practical examples.

In England, in Germany, and in Switzerland certain groups of young people resolved to bring pressure to bear on the multinational companies who had their headquarters in those countries. By getting together and making sacrifices they were able to buy a few shares in the companies. This entitled them to attend the annual general meetings. They got hold of complete lists of shareholders and sent letters to every one saying: "Dear Sir or Madam, like you we hold shares in this company.

As shareholders, like you we hope to make a profit from our investment. But we are sure that like us you do not wish to make a profit out of human suffering. So we would ask you to make every effort to attend this year's annual general meeting, at such and such a time and place, and give careful consideration to what we are going to say there, to the statistics and arguments that we are going to present." But of course the management of the companies quickly found a way of excluding the young protesters.

In Canada we began another experiment. I was invited there by the five largest Christian denominations in Canada, who every year organize what they call "Ten Days for Development." I told them about the young people's frustrated efforts in Europe and added: "Perhaps the major Christian denominations can succeed where these young people failed. The Christian churches very often invest in multinationals. It's quite understandable: they have to maintain churches and clergy, often subsidize social work, and finance missionary expansion; and in order to make sure that the money people give them does not lose its value, they have to invest it and invest it well. So they are enmeshed in the system. If you have money invested in multinational companies, I would ask you to leave it there for the time being. But you can take advantage of your position: ask for detailed information about how the company's profits are earned. It's far more difficult to get rid of the Christian churches than a group of young people. They have far more money, for one thing; and they have considerable moral influence. If the churches together obtain detailed information; if together they discover that the profits of major capitalist enterprises derive from the oppression of human beings, if together they draw conclusions from their findings — it must set off a worldwide movement for justice."

But perhaps it is still too soon to ask religious leaders to do this, even Christian leaders. Again, we must be patient and work at making them aware of the problem. This is what the Christians and other volunteers began to do in the United States in preparation for the bicentennial year, when they asked somewhat awkward questions about the justice and liberty that Americans vow to guarantee all men.

I distrust choices and decisions that are made in high places, without the participation of the people. Take the study of the "new international economic order," for example, which the United Nations has finally managed to set up. It's highly significant as it proves that something must be wrong with the current international economic order, otherwise we wouldn't be looking for a new one. But I'm quite sure it won't be long before the "experts" take over, the economic powers interfere, and the new international economic order will be conceived and defined from the top, without any assistance from the people. It will be a mockery of a new economic order: a new mask, in effect, for old imperialism. And the oppression will continue as before.

That is why we need the minorities to be present, vigilant, and active. And always hopeful. I cannot believe that a world created by a God who is love, liberated by the Son of God who is love, and sustained by the Holy Spirit who is love, will ever give itself up to selfishness and hatred. It's impossible!   — CB, 180–84

THE ROOTS OF RADICALISM

In the late 1970s Dom Helder described the process of radicalization that took place among the Brazilian bishops as follows:

We began to investigate social problems and to realize that the major conflict was not that between capitalism and communism, between East and West. Capitalism exploited the East-West conflict for its own ends, presenting itself — as it still presents itself now in Brazil, in fact in the whole of Latin America — as the savior of Christian civilization. That's total hypocrisy, as the roots of capitalism are entirely materialistic. It is irresponsible to make such claims. We wanted to face up to important human problems. We wanted people to realize that within our own country and continent there is the scandal of internal colonialism, and that on an international level there is the scandal of rich countries that maintain their wealth by keeping poor countries in misery. To say or think that what led us to side with the oppressed and the people was political considerations, a fear of losing their support, a desire to preserve our influence over them — no, no, it's impossible, because it's untrue. Absolutely untrue.

Our main concern was to make sure that the people would no longer be exploited. We were aware that we ourselves had manipulated the people; we had used them to defend a certain kind of morality, to defend what we had called religious principles, to defend the family against divorce for instance, and religious teaching in schools, and the presence of chaplains in the army and in hospitals. We had been so blinded then by the need to maintain, sustain, and support authority and social order that we couldn't see the terrible, cruel injustices that this authority and social order permitted. But as soon as we began to realize the truth and face up to it, we had to think and act in a different way.

And there were the encyclicals. If you look at the whole series of encyclicals, from Leo XIII to Paul VI, you find that each one is more stringent than the last on the subject of justice. But it's a pity, it's a pity that we Christians — Catholics and Protestants alike — are so intelligent, so strong when it comes to setting fine important principles down on paper, and so weak afterward, so timid and fearful when it comes to enacting those principles. And it isn't only the resistance, the opposition, the pressure from governments that prevents us enacting, for example, the remarkable conclusions of the Second Vatican Council. Very often it's the cautious advice from within our own ranks: "We must be patient! We mustn't go too fast!" The response to that must be: "I'm sorry! But the principles are here, the conclusions are here. We have discussed them at great length. We have agreed on them and ratified them. And it's not true to say we want to go too fast. Latin America has been waiting for four and a half centuries. And Africa, and Asia. . . . Why should we not preach revolution? Revolution to us doesn't mean violence and armed combat. It means the radical and swift change of unjust structures. It has nothing to do with the numerous revolutions Latin America has seen already, which have often resulted in a change of personnel, but never in a change of structures."

We aren't preoccupied with tactics. When we began to investigate social problems we realized the importance and urgency of human advancement. Human advancement is not like the advancement of a civil servant, say, who wants to move up from category G to category H! There are hundreds of millions of people in the world who are living in subhuman conditions. It's true that only they can raise themselves up: we can't do it for them. But we can and we must help them and encourage them. And first we have to defend them, to make sure that they are at least given the opportunity to raise themselves to a human condition. If only we could all dedicate ourselves to the cause of human advancement.

I'll tell you what finally opened our eyes. On the one hand, the reality that appeared more and more brutal; on the other, the teaching of the popes and the church contained in the encyclicals and the Second Vatican Council. And then the miracle of Pope John! How he reinforced our faith in the active presence of the Holy Spirit!

No one was expecting Pope John. Leo XIII, Pius X, Benedict XV, Pius XI, Pius XII. . . . There we were, listening to the radio, and asking ourselves: "Who will be elected, who will be chosen by providence to follow this wonderful succession of pontiffs?" And we were told that a certain Angelo Roncalli had been elected. He had chosen to be called John XXIII. An old man. . . .

In less than five years everything had changed, a complete revolution was under way. There's no human explanation. What a great day it was when this old man announced that the Holy Spirit had inspired him to summon an ecumenical council, and that he saw the reform of the church as a preliminary step to the union of all Christians! A great event!

So you see there was a whole series of things that brought about our change of attitude. We couldn't remain any longer as we had been, tied to the social order, to political power and the state.   — *CB,* 84–86

THE CHALLENGE

Is there anywhere in the world free from injustice, inequality, and division? Is there anywhere where injustice is not the primary violence breeding all other violence? Where violent protest against injustice, taking to the streets, does not threaten public order and the security of the state? And where it does not meet with violent repression by the authorities?

Almost everywhere there are many, particularly among the young, who have come to believe that the only way to do away with injustice is to rouse the victims of injustice, the oppressed, and organize them to fight for better days.

There are also many who want a juster and more human world but do not believe that force and armed violence are the best way of getting it. Those who choose active non-violence — the violence of the peaceful — do not need religion or ideology to see that the earth is ruled today by powerful combines, economic, political, technocratic, and military alliances. How would it be possible to beat these lords of the earth in armed combat when they have as their allies arms manufacturers and warmongers?

The difficult question then arises: what can be achieved by non-violence? Do the non-violent realize that the need is not just for a few small reforms but, in both the developed and the underdeveloped countries, the transformation of the political, cultural, economic, and social structures?

Yes. The non-violent do not in the least underestimate the difficulty of the task. If I may speak personally, I could mention my own half-failure, which forces me to struggle on and offers me new hopes.

I dreamed for six years of a large liberating moral pressure movement. I started Action for Justice and Peace. I traveled half the world. I appealed to institutions, universities, churches, religious groups, trade unions, technicians' organizations, youth movements, etc. After six years I concluded that institutions as such are unable to engage in bold and decisive action for two reasons: they can only interpret the average opinions of their members, and in capitalist society they have to be directly or indirectly bound up with the system in order to survive.

And although I now realize that it is virtually useless to appeal to institutions as such, everywhere I go, I find minorities with the power for love and justice that could be likened to nuclear energy locked for millions of years in the smallest atoms and waiting to be released.   —*DF*, 7–8

A MARVELOUS DISCOVERY

The essential thing is this marvelous discovery: that all over the world, among all races, languages, religions, ideologies, there are men and women born to serve their neighbor, ready for any sacrifice if it helps to build at last a really juster and more human world.

They belong in their own environment but they feel themselves to be members of the human family. They think of other people everywhere as their brothers and sisters, people from every latitude and longitude, every climate, people of all sizes and colors, rich or poor, whatever their education or their culture.

I beg you, let us try to understand this message with all good will. Let every minority make it its own and translate it into its own language.

I am from the West, a Latin American, a Christian. That is the language in which I clothe my thoughts, and I shall not change it. If you do not believe in God, do not be irritated when I refer to him, or to Christ, if you are not a Christian. Translate into your own language the truths I speak, which are not the creations of personal fantasy but realities experienced together by all those who belong to the same spiritual family.

Sometimes the text will suggest simple translations, simplified because we have decided to unite, knowing the time is short and the severe problems we face are daily becoming more severe. I will set out simply how I see our minorities, and why I think

they have essential work to do in the unification of mankind
and the establishment of lasting peace through love and justice.

—*DF*, 11

WE BLESS YOU, FATHER

We bless you, Father,
for the thirst
you put in us,
for the boldness
you inspire,
for the fire
alight in us,
that is you in us,
you the just.

Never mind
that our thirst
is mostly unquenched
(pity the satisfied).
Never mind
our bold plots
are mostly unclinched,
wanted not realized.

Who better than you
knows that success
comes not from us?
You ask us to do
our utmost only,
but willingly.

—*DF*, 9–10

MARGINALIZATION:
A UNIVERSAL PHENOMENON

Anyone who has stood by the road trying to hitch a ride in a hurry and watched the cars flash past him can understand what is meant by "marginal."

A marginal person is someone who is left by the wayside in the economic, social, political, and cultural life of his country.

We could imagine that in an underdeveloped country the whole population would be living in the same subhuman conditions. But this is not the case. What usually happens might be called an internal colonialism. Small groups of rich people live off the poverty of their fellow citizens.

These small local rich groups help the great rich foreigners. Some call them a "consular bourgeoisie" because they are like the consuls who used to be sent abroad to represent an empire or an emperor.

We could imagine that there are no marginal persons in developed countries. This is also false. Even in rich countries there are groups who remain poor. Remain marginal. They might be immigrants who have come to look for work, old-age pensioners, the unemployed.

Marginalization does not affect only groups or individuals. There exist today marginal countries or even continents. This is what we mean by the "third world," Africa, Asia, and Latin America.

The first development decade has come and gone. The rich countries have become richer and the poor countries have become poorer. Marginalization has increased.

The problem is more complicated than that because marginalization has at least three stages. At the first stage the marginal do not reap the benefits of economic progress. At the second stage they are deprived of productive power. At the third stage they are deprived of the power of decision.   —DF, 34–35

PUT YOUR EAR TO THE GROUND

Put your ear to the ground
and listen,
hurried, worried footsteps,
bitterness, rebellion.
Hope
hasn't yet begun.
Listen again.
Put out feelers.
The Lord is there.
He is far less likely
to abandon us
in hardship
than in times of ease.

—DF, 36

BEYOND CHARITY

We must go beyond "aid" or "charity" and demand justice that will bring peace. Many people falter at this point. He who asks the powerful to give aid to the poor, or helps the poor himself by being imprudent enough, or bold enough, to mention these or those rights or demand this or that justice, is regarded as a splendid man, a saint. But he who chooses to demand justice generally, seeking to change structures that reduce millions of God's children to slavery, must expect his words to be distorted, to be libeled and slandered, viewed with disfavor by governments, perhaps imprisoned, tortured, killed. . . . But this is the eighth beatitude: "Blessed are you when men revile you and persecute you and utter all kinds of evil against you falsely on my account. Rejoice and be glad for your reward is great in heaven, for so men persecuted the prophets who were before you." But is there any point in a peaceful demand for justice, even if this peaceful demand is firm and determined, when we are bound up and compromised in our daily life by the whole structure of injustice and oppression?

To the extent that we genuinely admit the contradiction, to the extent that we truly want to find the way out both for ourselves and the institutions to which we belong, it is an excellent thing to become involved on the side of truth and justice.

An enormous effort will be needed to create awareness in the marginalized masses, both in the developed and the underdeveloped countries, to prepare them to fight their way out of their subhuman situation, and also prepare them not simply to become as bourgeois and as selfish as those whom today they condemn.

An enormous effort is also needed to create awareness in those who are privileged, both in rich countries where there are poor groups that they allow to remain, and there is neocolonialism that they support whether they realize it or not, and in underdeveloped countries where the privileged create and profit from internal colonialism. It is very difficult to create awareness in the privileged. The teacher must have great virtue, be kind but truthful, gentle but firm.

But if the effort is not made the scandal will continue and the rich will go on getting richer and the poor poorer. The spiral of violence will get worse, injustice will increase, the resistance of the oppressed or the young in the name of the oppressed will continue and repression will become more and more brutal.

When will governments and the privileged understand that there can be no true peace until justice has been established?

—*DF*, 41–42

GOD'S VOICE TODAY

We are told that Abraham and other patriarchs heard the voice of God. Can we also hear the Lord's call? Isn't it pretentious to say this? Dangerously presumptuous?

We live in a world where millions of our fellow men live in inhuman conditions, practically in slavery. If we are not deaf we hear the cries of the oppressed. Their cries are the voice of God.

We who live in rich countries, where there are always pockets of underdevelopment and wretchedness, hear, if we want to hear, the unvoiced demands of those who have no voice and no hope. The pleas of those who have no voice and no hope are the voice of God.

Anyone who has become aware of the injustices caused by the unfair division of wealth, must, if he has a heart, listen to the silent or violent protests of the poor. The protests of the poor are the voice of God. If we look at the relations between the poor countries and the capitalist and communist empires, we see that today injustice is not only done by one man to another, or by one group to another, but by one country to another. And the voice of the countries suffering these injustices is the voice of God.

In order to rouse us God makes use even of radical and violent rebellion. How can we not feel the urgent need to act when we see young people — sincere in their desire to fight injustice, but with violent means that only call down violent repression — show such courage in prison and under torture that it is difficult to believe that they are sustained only by materialist ideals. He who has eyes to see and ears to hear must feel challenged: how can we remain mediocre and ineffective when we have our faith to sustain us?

Are we so deaf that we do not hear a loving God warning us that humanity is in danger of committing suicide? Are we so selfish that we do not hear the just God demanding that we do all we can to stop injustice from suffocating the world and driving it to war? Are we so alienated that we can worship God at our ease in luxurious temples, which are often empty in spite of all their liturgical pomp, and fail to see, hear, and serve God where he is present and where he requires our presence, among mankind, the poor, the oppressed, the victims of injustices in which we ourselves are often involved?

It is not difficult to hear God's call today in the world about us. It is difficult to do more than offer an emotional response, sorrow, and regret. It is even more difficult to give up our comfort, break with old habits, let ourselves be moved by grace and change our life, be converted.   — *DF,* 18–19

COME, LORD

Do not smile and say
you are already with us.
Millions do not know you and to us who do,
what is the difference?
What is the point of your presence
if our lives do not alter?
Change our lives, shatter our complacency.
Make your word flesh of our flesh,
blood of our blood
and our life's purpose.
Take away the quietness
of a clear conscience.
Press us uncomfortably.
For only thus
that other peace is made,
your peace.   —DF, 20

LORD, TRY US

There are those
whose being
is possession.
There are those
whose essence
is giving.
            —DF, 34

SETTING OUT ON THE ROAD

Setting out is first of all getting out of ourselves, breaking
through the shell of selfishness hardening us within our own
ego, to stop revolving around ourselves as if we were the center of everything, refusing to be ringed in by the problems of

our small world. However important these may be, mankind is more important, and our task is to serve mankind.

Setting out is not covering miles of land or sea, traveling faster than the speed of sound. It is first and foremost opening ourselves to other people, trying get to know them, going out to meet them.

Opening ourselves to ideas, including those with which we disagree, this is what the good traveler should do. Happy are they who understand the words, "If you disagree with me you have something to give me."

If those who are with you always agree with you before you open your mouth, they are not companions but shadows. When disagreement is not a form of systematic blocking, when it rises from a different vision, it can only enrich us.

It is possible to travel alone. But the good traveler knows that the journey is human life, and life needs company. "Companion" means, etymologically, the person who eats the same bread. Happy are they who feel they are always on the road and that every person they meet is their chosen companion. The good traveler takes care of his weary companions. He guesses when they lose heart. He takes them as he finds them, listens to them. Intelligently, gently, above all lovingly, he encourages them to go on and recover their joy in the journey.

To travel for the sake of traveling is not the true journey. We must seek a goal, envisage an end to the journey, an arrival.

But there are journeys and journeys. For the Abrahamic minorities, setting out means to get moving and help many others to get moving to make the world juster and more human.

—*DF*, 20–21

IF YOU DISAGREE WITH ME

If you disagree with me,
you have something to give me,
if you are sincere
and seek the truth

as best you may,
honestly, with modest care,
your thought is growth
to mine, correction,
you deepen my vision.

—*DI*, 22

YOU ARE HEMMED IN

If you want to be free of yourself
you must build a bridge over the gulf
of loneliness your selfishness
has found, and look beyond.
Listen to another, and especially,
try loving him or her and not just "me."

—*DF*, 22

YOU WANT TO BE

You want to be,
excuse me,
first get free
of that excess
of goods
which cram
your whole body
leaving no room
for you and even less
for God.

—*DF*, 23

BECOME AN EXPERT

Become an expert
in the art
of discovering the good
in every person.
No one
is entirely bad.
Become an expert
in the art
of finding the truthful core
in views of every kind.
The human mind
abhors total error.
— *DF*, 28

ABRAHAMIC MINORITIES, UNITE!

God could have chosen many ways of sharing his gifts. He could have shared them with strict equality. No one would have reason for complaint, no one would have more or less. Everything would have been calculated, adjusted, balanced.... But this would be unworthy of the Father's creative imagination. It would be incredibly monotonous, as if all human beings had exactly the same face, or all flowers were the same shape and color and smelled the same....

God accepts the risk of appearing to be unjust. At least he does not refuse anyone the indispensable. But some have gifts heaped upon them. I am speaking here of true riches, the riches of the personality. There are people who are rich in divine gifts and privileged by divine grace. God looks unjust, but he is not. He asks more from those to whom he gives more. They are not greater or better, they have greater responsibility. They must give more service. Live to serve.

Some people will now hurriedly insist — but without great conviction or sincerity — that they have barely the essentials, etc. But it is a waste of time to weigh up and measure gifts in this way. It is not important whether we have been given much or little. What matters is to make a firm decision to make the best possible use of them and to serve.

God thinks of all people but calls some to special work. He drives these to take a leap in the dark, to set out. He tries them by fearful hardships. But he supports and encourages them. He gives them the fine and dangerous mission to act as his instruments. He entrusts them with the task of being present discreetly when decisive decisions are made. He sends them out on the road to draw others to them, many others. He expects them to bear witness in the hour of trial.

Abraham was the first to be thus called by God. He did not delay for a moment. He set out. He faced hardships. He learned to his cost how to arouse his brothers in the name of God. To call. To encourage. To start moving.

Jews, Christians, and Muslims know the story of the father of believers. What is his name in the other great religions? Did Abraham receive great gifts? He gave a faithful return, the best he could. He served. Will those who are not Jews or Christians or Muslims allow us to give Abraham's name to those minorities who are called to serve? Of course other races and religions can use an equivalent name that is more appropriate to their tradition.

And you, my brothers who are atheist humanists, don't think you have been forgotten. Translate what I say in my language into your language. When I talk of God, translate, perhaps by "nature," "evolution," what you will.

If you feel in you the desire to use the qualities you have, if you think selfishness is narrow and choking, if you hunger for truth, justice, and love, you can and should go with us. Even if you don't know it, or perhaps don't want to know, you are our brother or sister. Accept our friendship. We will learn to understand each other and we will be able to go forward together.   —*DF,* 12–14

HAVE YOU NOTICED
WHO BURY THEIR TALENTS?

Not just the man with only one,
but people given five or ten,
instead of reaping double,
become comfortable,
falsely cautious,
falsely humble,
and at harvest home return
in empty-handed barrenness.
Don't call them yet to account.
Wait a moment.
Let me go out
to my brothers, try
to rouse them by my cry.
— *DF*, 14

HOPE WITHOUT RISK

Hope without risk
is not hope,
which is believing
in risky loving,
trusting others
in the dark,
the blind leap
letting God take over.
— *DF*, 15

THE VIOLENCE OF THE TRUTH

If you feel you belong in spirit to the family of Abraham, do
not wait for permission to act. Don't wait for official action
or new laws. The family of Abraham is more a spirit than an

institution, more a lifestyle than an organization. It requires the minimum of structure and depends only on a few general principles.

The minimum of structure: anyone who feels he belongs to the family of Abraham should not remain alone. Make an effort to find someone, near at hand or further away, who already belongs to this family or who could belong. Make contact. How? That depends on the situation. The essential thing is to get out of isolation. There are no rules about the formation of groups, number of members, form that meetings should take. You are brothers meeting to help each other fight discouragement and develop the necessary faith, hope and love.

The first thing to do is to look and listen, get information on the situations in which the Abrahamic minorities could be involved. Won't that be a big job? No. Any member of the Abrahamic minorities can find out about what is happening around him, in the neighborhood where he lives or at work.

He must discover where the worst injustices are, the worst exhibitions of selfishness, from the local to the international scale. Every member of the family of Abraham, according to his opportunities, will be able to get much more detailed and human information than can be gathered from the official statistics.

In underdeveloped countries the Abrahamic minorities must try to find out and understand what is involved in a subhuman situation. "Subhuman" is an explosive word. Take it in detail. Find out about housing. Do the places where some people live deserve to be called houses? Do they afford the necessary minimum of comfort to a human life? How many people are there per room? Look at the water, drains, electricity, the floor, the roof. Investigate clothing, food, health, work, transport, leisure in the same way. Pictures can be helpful. Take photographs and so on. But you must also turn to statistics to discover whether this is an isolated case or the general condition. You should ask the right questions. With work, for example, does it pay a living wage sufficient to support a family, is employment guaranteed or are there frequent layoffs? Are trade unions encouraged, tolerated, interfered with, forbidden? What are the apprenticeship conditions? The sanitary conditions? Holidays? Retirement provisions? Are the laws on social conditions followed? Are human beings treated with respect?

This sort of inquiry could of course arouse suspicion, and that could have unpleasant consequences. But it is necessary to find out what the real situation is in conditions of internal colonialism.

What other way is there of becoming convinced and of convincing others of the huge gap between those who operate and those who suffer from an almost feudal situation in which the masses have no voice and no hope? Such information would not aim at inciting anger and rebellion but at providing a solid argument for the necessity to change the structures.

We should not forget the extreme cases where it would be necessary to prove that an apparently patriarchal regime is in fact a cover for absolute dominion over life and death, for a master who can give and take at will, allow or forbid the provision and maintenance of houses, the cultivation of a small strip of land and the keeping of a few cattle, literacy, trade unionism, etc.

How are we to find out about the price paid by sweated workers, slaves innumerable, for profits to those who put their money in foreign banks in secret numbered accounts?

How can we find out about abuses of economic power on the national and international scale? Where can we find figures for what official statistics do not disclose, for the illegal export of profits that are blood, sweat, and tears?

Must we repeat it? Such information does not aim to provoke hatred or subversion. Its aim is to supply liberating moral pressure. For many, this in itself is dangerous and subversive. But one day it will be understood that this violence of the peaceful is greatly preferable to the explosion of armed violence.

In developed countries the Abrahamic minorities must also investigate and try to understand, for example:

- The existence of underdevelopment (gray zones) in rich countries, and what this means in terms of human misery.

- The injustices in trade between developed and underdeveloped countries.

- The difference between the aid figures for poor countries and the figures for the losses made by these countries because the price of raw materials is kept so low that they cannot pay for the manufactured goods they have to buy.

- The inhuman and criminal sale or gift of arms to poor countries under the pretext that these aid development, involving these poor countries in dangerous and ridiculous arms races and increasing local poverty.

- Details of the reality of economic power...

It would be humiliating to admit that one was unable to gather such information. The challenge must be accepted.

Choosing the way of moral pressure is not choosing the easy way out. We are replacing the force of arms by moral force, the violence of the truth. We must believe that love can strengthen the courage and the numbers of these Abrahamic minorities who want justice but who refuse to answer violence with violence.

Love will find the way to rouse and organize these minorities in all human groups.

Love will find the best way to unite without uniformity these various non-violent movements so that they can help each other.

Love will enable them to find in their religion or even in atheist humanism steadfastness in the fight for the peaceful liberation of oppressed peoples all over the world, whatever the consequences.

Love will help them to decide firmly that the goal is not superficial reform but the transformation of inhuman structures, to find methods that although they are non-violent are useful and effective in bringing about this transformation.

In their work of diagnosing unjust situations, in their action of liberating moral pressure these minorities must be careful to remain humble. As we know our own selfishness, we must be aware that if we were in the place of those we condemn, we might behave in the same way as they do. Our family, our group or church may also bear some of the responsibility for those situations that we have decided peacefully but decisively to change. —*DF*, 47–51

JOIN TOGETHER

Stone, brick, and tile
together all
compose
the house.
Unbuilt the pile
of single elements
are the hope
of a house.
But more important
is to plan and put it up.
The building done
is greater than
the unassembled material.
—*DF*, 51

ANONYMOUS HEROISM

Forgive me if I disturb your peace of mind. But why not ask yourself today, without wasting time deciding whether you have received little or much, whether you have been given the wonderful but awkward, great but dangerous vocation to serve humanity as a member of the Abrahamic minorities?

If we are to understand the potential force of these minorities, we must realize the value of each man however "average" he may be. It would be easy to discount such a man, who is neither a great saint nor a great sinner, incapable either of great cowardice or great courage. He wants to live in peace with his own family. We are tempted to apply to him the terrible words of the Bible: he is neither cold nor hot. God will spew him out of his mouth.

If it is true that the average man is not made for heroism or martyrdom, it is also true that his daily life is made up of sacrifices and acts of anonymous heroism.

The taxi driver in a small provincial town who provides for the education of his eight children. The clerical worker's wife who performs miracles of organization to add to her husband's salary what they need for their two children and the third one on the way. The girl who does not marry but adopts eleven nephews, who are the children of her two brothers.... In the Middle Ages this was called "white martyrdom." We could give endless examples of it.

These are the people whose sacrifice is their daily grind. Are there others who could take on the problems of the larger human family? The average man lives monotonously: the same house, the same faces, the same voices, the same worries. These others give themselves without stint. They accept the burden and they do not remain anonymous.

It would be stupid and unjust to despise the average man, who is after all in the majority. We should try to form an alliance between him and the front-line fighters. We should recognize, truly not just as a tactical maneuver, the value of anonymous heroism, white martyrdom.

If we give him his due, the average man will readily see for his part that others might have a different vocation and see also that there might be ways in which he could help the work of these minorities. If he is understood, informed, listened to, and roused to peaceful violence, this average man could play a vital part.   —*DF*, 51–53

ITS OWN FUNCTION

Bolt and nut
are as essential
in the job they do
as a head of state
to avert harm.
Both fail too.
— *DF*, 53

DO NOT FORGET

In a fabulous necklace
I had to admire
the anonymous string
by which the whole thing
was strung together.
— *DF*, 53

ARE INSTITUTIONS HOPELESS?

One of the temptations that face the Abrahamic minorities is the fear that the structures of which they are part make it impossible for them to have any real effect in changing the world. They are tempted because they do not feel they are better than other people.

For example, priests or nuns who want to follow the spirit of Vatican II or bring into effect the conclusions of the Latin American bishops' conference at Medellín should not be astonished if they feel misunderstood by their brothers and sisters. They would be yielding to temptation if they decided to leave their community and give way to dangerous bitterness.

Instead of feeling beaten, instead of quitting and imagining how to reform the institution from the outside, would it not be better to think that within the institution itself and in all sorts of places there are others who are in the middle of the very same experience? Why not seek an intelligent and effective way, which would also be loyal and constructive, of contacting all these others who are also anxious to serve their neighbor better? I do not mean condemning those who are more conservative or plotting against them. I mean you need not feel isolated, you need not be discouraged, when you are trying to revitalize the institution itself from within.

Of course you will risk being misunderstood. However pure your intentions you will look like a rebel. Perhaps you will be punished. This is excellent training for attacking and overcoming socio-economic and politico-cultural structures. You will be able to take the measure of your courage, prudence, loyalty, kindness, power of decision, and responsibility....

We all should realize that there are other young people and adults everywhere who want what we want....There are Abrahamic minorities everywhere who are only waiting for the signal to begin and to unite.   —*DF,* 44–46

SO YOU THINK THAT

So you think that
because of her weaknesses,
Christ will forsake her?
The worse his church and ours
is marred by our failures,
the steadier he will support her
with his tender care.
He could not deny
his own body.   —*DF,* 46

THE HARMONIST

I admire and envy
your rare ear,
true to each note
discerning falsity
however slight.
And even more
your mastery,
blending the dissonant
into harmony.
— *DF*, 46

TO ARTISTS

The artist cannot be judged by the measure of ordinary mortals. He shares more directly in the creating power of the Father. Everything in him is unexpected and original. He bridles against regulation, monotony, routine.

The artist is usually open to the human values of justice and freedom. He cannot breathe the air of dictatorship. He is ultra-sensitive and feels the coming future. He speaks (each in his proper language, poetry, theater, cinema, painting, sculpture, music) in the name of others who cannot speak.

By definition artists belong to the Abrahamic minorities. If an artist does not care about the construction of a more human world, he must have become bourgeois and sold to avarice, ambition, and selfishness.

What can be expected from committed artists in the Abrahamic minorities? They should be so thoroughly aware of the great problems facing mankind and the greatest injustices that it automatically comes out in their work.

Poets helped to condemn black slavery. Poets, slavery still goes on! More than two-thirds of mankind are slaves to hunger, sickness, forced labor, despair. And the other third is in slavery to selfishness and fear.

Popular music bears the message further than the most learned scientific treatises. What the people sing speaks to the mind and imagination of both singer and listener.

Theater has been and always will be powerful. It is indispensable for the work of making people more aware of the situation, particularly if it reaches the common people.

The cinema is the medium with the greatest impact on the masses because it is pictorial. Good documentaries can have great power.

Humor is a subtle and effective instrument. There are situations where in practice there is nothing to be done but make people laugh and the oppressors often do not understand what the laughter is about....

We could continue this list. What is essential is that the artist should be a genuine artist. He should not be a mere propagandist. That would debase his work. His message should be flesh of his flesh and blood of his blood.   —DF, 54–55

THE JUDGMENT

When on judgment day
the angels call the artists in,
they will be so proud
of their share
in God the Father's power
of creation,
that the Son
will find it hard
to judge them strictly,
because poets especially
remind him of his Father.
                          —DF, 56

TO ATHEIST HUMANISTS

Not long ago people wondered whether atheists could really exist. How would it be possible for the creature to do without God? Isn't atheism simply snobbery that vanishes in a crisis? "I am an atheist, thank God" goes the oft-quoted phrase. But today there can be no doubt that atheists exist throughout the world. There are people who do not believe in God for the simple reason that they feel no need of him, either in their thoughts or their actions, their private or public life, their easy or their hard times.

This calm atheism is considerably more serious than the old-fashioned militant and aggressive kind, which often sounded like bitter resentment of God. We often hear of the death of God. For many the expression simply means the death of a concept of God made in the image and likeness of men. As our idea of God becomes purer, the simple faith of the child must grow into the more enlightened vision of the adult. Those who reject God in the name of science may one day discover that the mind can seek outside the boundaries of science without betraying itself. Those who get rid of God because they consider him incompatible with the freedom of man may one day see that it is possible to think of man as a co-creator who is able to free himself from slavery.

We do not want to argue about the existence of God here. We see that there are people who are atheists who are also humanists and concerned with the human person, liberation, and development. A believer might say that the phrase "atheistic humanism" is sort of double atheism. It both denies the existence of God and puts man in the place of God. But those who have anything to do with humanists realize that this is not the case. For the believer the law is to love God and his neighbor. Anyone who loves his neighbor is already fulfilling half the law. Anyone who truly loves his neighbor must also love, without knowing it, the Creator and Father.

We all know that people, often young people, become atheists because believers, particularly believers in positions of responsibility, disappoint them when they do not practice what they preach.

Some atheist humanists are very impressive. They love truth, justice, and peace, they are willing to serve and give of their utmost, they are brave and resist suffering and torture; they are examples to the believer.

We who are believers can say that any man who lives the truth and who has the courage to work for peace in this way will see God.

And in any case in the work of the Abrahamic minorities atheist humanists have a crucial part. They are usually respected not only by young atheists but also by believers who have their doubts and problems. An atheist humanist can be of the greatest help to the Abrahamic minorities. He can give an example of the gift of his time and reputation for the cause of justice on the way to peace. He can rouse unbelievers or doubters to shake off their indifference and leave their ease to risk the construction of a better world. He can find in his very atheism reasons to convince himself and others why they should become involved in the struggle against injustice, marginalization, and slavery.   —DF, 56–58

Atheists and Christians should revise their views of each other. Belief in God does not necessarily make men slaves. Many atheists can share the belief in man as co-creator.

In any case education for freedom cannot do without the help of atheists, and Christians should realize that atheist humanism shows an effective love for mankind.

Religions are uniting to show that love of men is a special way of loving God. They are trying to preach the Gospel both to the poor who have been made subhuman by their living conditions, so that they may know the truth that will help them get rid of their poverty, and to the rich, who have become inhuman through their excesses, so that they may know the truth that will help them become human again. They try to denounce selfishness as the great evil and unmask it at the local, regional, national, and international levels.   —DF, 39

IN TE SPERAVI SEMPER

This speaker
was not born within your fold,
supported by your grace,
held fast, never
to turn from you his face.

Hear the voice
of those who in all honesty
feel bound to choose
the cold
outside your house.

Nevertheless,
they still believe in you,
although they may not know it,
for are not you the truth?
And these people both
speak it and (in your own phrase)
do it.

You are beauty
and pure eyes remaining childlike
still look
wonderingly
on your earth's loveliness.

You are goodness
and I find you
in people who do not confess you.
They lack your body
but speak your mind.

            —*DF*, 58–59

THE PRAYER OF
THE FAMILY OF ABRAHAM

Some believe in and rely on prayer; others think of it as mumbo jumbo. But we should not allow the word "prayer" to divide us. Whenever we express our dearest wishes, that is praying.

What prayer could the Abrahamic minorities say in common, over and above their differences?

Let us open our eyes. Let us begin at once to fight our selfishness and come out of ourselves, to dedicate ourselves once and for all, whatever the sacrifices, to the non-violent struggle for a more just and more human world.

Let us not put off the decision till tomorrow. Let us begin today, now, intelligently and firmly.

Let us look about us and recognize our brothers and sisters who are called like us to give up their ease and join all those who hunger for the truth and who have sworn to give their lives to make peace through justice and love.

Let us not waste time discussing who shall be our leader. What is important is for us to unite and go forward, remembering that time too is our enemy.

Let us give the best of ourselves to helping create moral pressure for freedom to bring about the necessary structural changes.

Let us gather information on the situations we wish to change.

Let us spread this information by all reasonable means at our disposal. And let the information be truthful, able to stand up to criticism and disturb the consciences of all good men.

Let us through all this stand firm without falling into hatred, let us be understanding without conniving at evil.

—*DF,* 62–63

DO NOT FEAR THE TRUTH

Do not fear the truth.
hard as it may appear,
grievously as it may hurt,
it is still right
and you were born for it.
If you go out to meet
and love it,
let it exercise your mind,
it is your best friend
and closest sister.

— *DF,* 28

TO THE END

No, do not give in.
Grace divine was your good beginning.
That grace is greater that does not falter.
But the greatest
is to keep going
however
you are undermined, to endure,
however harassed
to the end.

— *DF,* 29

3

Walking with God

DOM HELDER'S RELIGION

One of the best descriptions of Dom Helder's religious outlook, which deals with the paradox of a shrewd political operator who could also speak tenderly to an ant, is by a friend and colleague from Recife, Zildo Rocha:

> His religious life consisted basically in taking seriously and living deeply a few simple, basic truths of the Christian faith:
>
> - God is Creator and Father.
>
> - Jesus is the firstborn among his brothers and sisters.
>
> - Mary is Jesus' mother and ours.
>
> - The human race is one big family, of which all of us, without exception, form part.
>
> - The immense family of human beings extends into and is complemented by another family of angelic spirits, that give it company, help, and protection.
>
> - The central act in which the human and angelic families meet the Father is the holy Mass, understood not as the ritual of a specific sect, but as a cosmic and universal act in which Christ, the Priest of Creation,

gathers together and brings to perfection in himself all things, and takes them back, in the Spirit, to the Father.

It is impossible to understand Dom Helder's life outside this basic framework of belief. From the experience of the Creator and Father, which filled him with confidence and optimism, he drew an intimacy of love and submission to God and an almost spontaneous passion for the universe, an enchantment with nature, a tenderness for plants and animals, with whom, although a viscerally urban man, he regularly communicated on the wings of imagination and contemplation, as proved by the poems and meditations that flowed from his vigils.

But anyone who drew from this description the idea that Dom Helder's religion was a refuge or a metaphysical cloud in which to find shelter from the vicissitudes of history and the world would be making a great mistake. It is no less true to say that Dom Helder could never understand religious life and mission dissociated from social and political action. He never believed in religious practice that didn't have an impact and repercussion on society, on its political and social structure.[1]

The extent to which this religion permeated Dom Helder's life comes across in these texts. He describes himself as "always seeing the unclouded Christ," a claim that might seem monstrous arrogance were it not tempered by the humor that runs through his conversation. But his deep conviction of God's love is what enabled him to be understanding about the marital difficulties of so many of his flock, and to take a relaxed attitude toward the mixture of African religion and Christianity that is such a striking feature of Brazilian Catholicism.

Many of the texts in this chapter come from a series of interviews carried out by the French journalist Roger Bourgeon in the early 1980s and published as Through the Gospel with Dom

---

1. Rocha, *Helder, o Dom*, 210.

Helder Camara. *Bourgeon's description of Dom Helder during the interviews captures this living in the presence of God:*

> For three or four hours each day you would come and sit in the parlor of some nuns you had asked to put us up. We would read a passage aloud. You would sit quite still listening with your eyes shut. Then after a moment's silence you would open your eyes and, with your hands raised in a gesture we soon came to know well, begin to speak. Oblivious of the mike and video-recorder. Dom Helder talked about and — I think — often with the Lord.[2]

What's the point of talking about Jesus today?

D.H.: Because this Man changed history. He is alive in history. At every step I meet him every day. And I meet him in the flesh. He said, whoever is suffering, humiliated, crushed is he. In our own times when more than two-thirds of the human race are living in subhuman conditions, it's easy enough to meet him in the flesh.

Was Jesus exactly as the evangelists say he was? I'm no biblical critic. I'm not against biblical criticism, but I prefer to let the critics get on with their own discussions. For my part I am as sure of Christ's existence as I am of my own hand with its five fingers I can touch and see. I meet Jesus every day. And we are one. No doubt about it.

But was there any particular moment when you discovered this?

Like a child discovering it has feet. It's always known it's got feet, but one day it discovers them.

At a given moment, certainly, I became aware of Christ's presence in those who suffer, and of his presence inside myself. When? I don't know. I was brought up in a family that was Christian not so much by label as in actions. My father and mother didn't practice their religion very regularly. Who gave me the idea of becoming a priest when I was still a little boy? What did this desire amount to in my childish mind?

---

2. Roger Bourgeon, in his introduction to *Through the Gospel with Dom Helder Camara* (Maryknoll, N.Y.: Orbis Books, 1986), 3.

Anyhow, one day my father asked me this question: "You keep saying you want to be a priest. But do you really understand what being a priest involves?" He then sketched the ideal priest in terms exactly corresponding to what I felt without understanding, to what I dreamed though unable to put it into words: "My boy, priest and self-centeredness don't go together. That's impossible. A priest isn't his own master. He has only one reason for living: to live for others."

This corresponded precisely to what the Lord had already sown in my heart. All my life I've lived the dream of being one with Christ to help my fellow-beings conquer their self-centeredness.

You speak to Jesus. Does he speak to you?
Christ speaks to all of us. He is here.

But do you hear him speaking?
Whenever you listen to someone who is suffering, you hear Christ's voice. And whenever you meet someone suffering, you meet him in person.

In one of your books you say that every night, during your "vigil," as you call it, you talk to Jesus.
There's no need to talk; thinking is enough. During my "vigil" I try to recover unity with Christ. And with him I relive the meetings of the past day. I think, for instance, about the mother who told me about the problems she has with her husband, with her children, and how hard she finds it to feed them. And, through this very real mother whom I know by name, I think about all the mothers throughout the world throughout the ages: the poor ones, the rich ones, the happy ones, the unhappy ones. Or I think about the man I saw working in the street, emptying dustbins. I had caught his eye. He didn't dare offer me his hand. I virtually had to force him: "Work isn't what soils our hands, friend. No hand was ever soiled by work. Self-centeredness is what soils them." This man, Francisco or Antonio as he may be, reminds me of working men throughout the world throughout the ages. Then I say to Christ our brother,

"Lord, two thousand years after your death injustices are growing worse and worse." Reviewing the day like this, I find time passes very quickly.

Do you feel this presence of Jesus constantly within you? Or are there absences, silences, gaps from time to time?

Occasionally on receiving a small favor, one might be tempted to think of it as one's due. But when the favor is an enormous one, it's harder to imagine one might have deserved it; one can't be tempted to vanity then.

I say this in connection with the favor the Lord has done me of always being so immediately present in me, in us, in our neighbor in a general sense, but most particularly in those who suffer. So present that very often when I'm thinking ahead to encounters that, were I on my own, I should find worrying, tiring, or irritating, as for instance when I have to advise someone or tell someone off, I say, "Lord, be one with me. Listen with my ears, look through my eyes, speak by my lips. I don't know what to say. Speak. I lend you my lips. Let my presence be your presence, Lord." That's what I do.

At Rio, right on the top of Mount Corcovado, stands a vast statue of Christ. Very often it's hidden in the clouds, and I think, "Lord, some of our brothers and sisters are suffering so frightfully, they think you have vanished from their lives, that you're hiding, that you aren't there any more. I know you're there, but they can't discover you anywhere."

When I consider the enormous responsibility entailed in always seeing the unclouded Christ, I can't impute this to any merit or righteousness of my own. Then I pray for those who are in the fog and can't see anything: "Don't you worry, Christ is there. These are only clouds, but he's there all the same. The clouds will go away, and then you will see for yourselves, the Lord is there."   — *TTG,* 5–7

But by baptism, by sanctifying grace, we are made sharers in the Lord's holiness. This isn't a favor reserved for the few. It's a gift and an obligation for us all. And being holy doesn't mean

having visions or working miracles. It means living by sanctifying grace, constantly mindful that we carry Christ within us
and that we walk within God.

One day I was taking viaticum to an invalid. This was in Rio
de Janeiro. The tram was packed. I kept my feet as best I could.
I was carrying Christ. On the tram there was a woman with
her children. I looked at them; it was Christ looking at them.
There were workmen, a very pretty girl: it was Christ looking at
them. Eventually I reached the sick man's house. After hearing
his confession, I gave him the host, the eucharistic Christ. And
then, for a few seconds, I was tempted to think, "How dreary
the return journey's going to be! I shall be all on my own.... "
But then I thought. "No. you won't! True, you won't be carrying Christ in the Eucharist any more, but the Lord will still be
there, ever present."

So, being holy isn't an exceptional privilege. How can we get
angry if the God of goodness is within us? How can we be jealous if the Lord is with us? How can we be selfish if the God of
compassion and sharing is there?   — *TTG*, 44

CHRIST'S AGONY

We often forget that the Son of God, true God like the Father and the Holy Spirit, is also true human being, like any
other human creature. Here we see the Son of God experienc-
ing very human fear (Luke 22:39–46). I love this passage. It's
encouraging. It shows that we too have a right to be afraid, to
be weak.

You know, no one can foretell how he will react to pain or
torture. In my experience those who appear the toughest before-
hand are the ones who sometimes turn out to be weaker. The
ones who stand firm are often the ones who were afraid, who
had no faith in themselves.

We are not born for pain or death. We are born for life
and joy.

I can also grasp that in Christ's agony there was not only the anguish of physical pain and approaching death. There was also the vision of the world and the world's sins: self-centeredness in particular, which is the greatest sin of all, and the consequences flowing from self-centeredness. He saw that, his sacrifice notwithstanding, self-centeredness would go on crushing thousands on thousands of millions of human creatures.

I don't underplay the human fear of martyrdom, but there was also his terrible sadness as God's envoy.

—*TTG*, 139–40

THE HOLY SPIRIT

The Holy Spirit is here! Almost tangibly! To know God the Father, you only have to look at the creation. There are moments when the Creator is almost visible. It's almost impossible to look at the creation without instantly becoming aware that the Creator is here, alive in it.

The Son of God, he too is here, in our neighbor and in ourselves.

As for the Holy Spirit. Ah, if you were with the poor, for instance in a pastoral movement we call "Brotherly Encounter," and were to ask who founded the movement, the immediate answer you'd get would be: "the Holy Spirit." You might expect them to say it was some bishop or priest. But no: "It was the Holy Spirit."

Now I'm going to tell you a true story. There was a woman who had taken on the job of going around to see her neighbors and encouraging them to stand firm, since they all knew they were threatened with eviction; some great man had bought the land where they were living. She kept saying, "They can't evict us like this: We're God's creatures, God's children. There's such a thing as human rights, you know!" But at a given moment she found the police at her door and coming into her house. "Dom Helder, I was trembling," she told me. For she knew the police don't behave the same way to the poor as they do to the rich. The poor have no resources, no lawyers, to defend them. "I was trembling," she went on. "I was simply panic-stricken especially when the policemen threw me into the van. Then I said, "Lord, you promised us if we were dragged into court, the Holy Spirit would be with us." I was still trembling. I was ice-cold with fear. But when I appeared before the big landlord who was to interrogate me, I felt the warmth coming back. It was the Spirit of God. I gave amazing, devastating answers. I couldn't begin to tell you now what they were, they were so good!"

That's how we know the Holy Spirit is here, present, alive. Never tell me it's hard to visualize the Holy Spirit. The Holy Spirit is our contemporary, living with us, helping us. What could our weakness do in moments of crisis, were it not for the strength of the Spirit of God?   — *TTG,* 26–27

I love the passage where Christ says, "Don't worry. The Spirit of your Father will do the talking."

Years ago when I was still in the seminary, I used to think this prophecy of the Lord's applied only to the early centuries of Christianity, to the persecutions recorded in church history. But clearly these words are valid for all time. Always, in every corner of the globe, you risk making enemies if you really try to live the Gospel.

Because the Gospel explodes self-centeredness. If you make up your mind, with the Lord's grace, to live the Gospel, that is to say, to oppose self-centeredness, you will inevitably run into trouble. With yourself and with other people. And not only with governments and powerful individuals, but with churchmen too. And not only with people, but with structures.

It makes me think of one of my priests who was worse than killed; he was butchered, for working for justice with the young. If someone the night before had said, "Dom Helder, tomorrow one of your priests is going to be sacrificed, murdered, tomorrow you'll have a martyr among your priests," I should certainly have run through the list of all my priests and tried to guess which of them was to be the chosen one. I could have thought of a dozen, maybe twenty. But I doubt if I should ever have thought of the one the Lord did in fact choose. He was such a modest, candid, simple soul.

Honestly, we don't need to worry about whether we shall have the strength, the courage, and the right words to say at the right moment. The strength will not come from us. And the answers will be those of the Spirit of the Father speaking in us.

— *TTG*, 70–71

The amazing thing, the surprising thing, thanks to the Holy Spirit who upholds and heartens the oppressed, is that to this very day I have never heard anyone saying: "O Son of God, you've got everything, while we are merely Cinderella-like stepchildren of God."

We have no right to abuse this patience of our people. Faith and the Holy Spirit teach us to do much more than we have; we must go beyond just working "for" the people and start working "with" the people.

It is the Holy Spirit who guarantees the authenticity of the local church groups and it is he who enables even the uneducated to teach and to prove that no one is born to be a slave or a beggar.

The slogan "The people united will never be defeated," is thus realized and it takes on a truer, more Christian dimension: *A people united and organized, a people united and relying on the grace of God, will rise up from poverty without hatred or violence, but with decision and courage.*

It is true that the tempter exists. He will do his utmost to create the maximum of confusion, but the divine Spirit will always give us his strength and his light.   — *SE*, 68–70

> Holy breathing of God,
> I feel you stirring.
> Warmed by this breath good things start to grow.
> Even in strong, wealthy lands
> fresh, mobilizing calls evoke planetary piety,
> winning the hearts and the hands of the caring:

> each in her chosen path,
> each with his special gift,
> take their stand
> to create a world more fit for living,
> more just and more humane.
>
> — *ML*, 37

GUARDIAN ANGELS

Materialism? What do you mean by that? I see matter as something living. In its own way it speaks, it sings, it prays. And it is holy, since everything that exists has either been created directly by the Lord or has been created by the Creator working through the co-creator, the human race. How well I understand Teilhard de Chardin when he dives into the heart of the matter and discovers it to be alive!

So you see no frontiers between matter, life, and spirit?

No, no frontiers. I find it is just as easy to pray to the Lord when I'm looking at a child smiling, or the sun rising, or a jet passing overhead. Because these are all part of creation.

I can well imagine many people find it hard to believe in angels. But I don't find it difficult at all. In the created world I see minerals, vegetables, animals, humanity. And between humanity and God, it seems to me, there is room for creatures which are our brothers and sisters as regards the spirit but do not have heavy bodies like ours.

I am on such familiar terms with my brothers the angels and am so convinced the Lord helps the human race by means of angels that I have given my own angel a name. It's not his proper name — at the moment I don't know what his real name is — but it makes him more real to me. I have given him the name my mother used to call me when she was very pleased with me. "Keep it up, José!" she would say. That's the name I have given my angel. And I can already imagine how happy

I shall be when, having reached the Father's house, I meet my angel and hear him tell me what his real name is.

You are all entitled to smile at me and my simplicity. But I can tell you this: traveling along with José my angel keeps me going, keeps my spirits up. Naturally I don't keep praying to my angel all the time over every petty problem. But in those most difficult, most critical moments, when there is no more human help to be had, then I ask my angel to protect me: "José, José, I know you're always there to help me. Help me! Better still, help me to help!" Never has he failed me. Never.

It's funny. I must confess I've never seen an angel. Not even my own angel. But that he's present is absolutely clear to me. I'm absolutely convinced he is.

One time in Rome, just once.... This was during the Holy Year in 1950. In those days we didn't yet have concelebration in the Western church. Each priest had to say "his own" Mass. We used to queue up to say Mass. This particular day I arrived early at one of the churches in Rome to say Mass. But I couldn't see where to stand so as to get to the head of the queue. Some fellow-priest was always slipping in ahead of me.

By this time it was almost midday. There was a good Franciscan brother there, getting the altar ready and serving each Mass. When he thought he'd finished with the last priest, he suddenly noticed I was still waiting my turn. Thinking you've already finished and then finding out that you haven't can make you cross. It made him cross. So I said, "Never mind, Brother, I'll come tomorrow. The Lord has seen I intended saying Mass today. I'll say it tomorrow." "No, no, no!" he said. And he got the altar ready. However, he kept one question up his sleeve: "Who, may I ask, is going to serve your Mass?" There always had to be someone else there besides the priest. "Don't worry. My angel will serve the Mass." "My angel?" ... Whereupon ... I can't explain it. Perhaps it was something to do with the electricity. There was such a brilliant light in the church that the poor Franciscan fell on his knees. He wept, he trembled, he trembled, he wept. I didn't want him to stay and serve my Mass.

But he did stay, trembling like a leaf and weeping right through the celebration.

Some people, because they don't believe in miracles, produce such complicated explanations that these are more supernatural than the supernatural itself. — *TTG*, 11–12

THE GOSPEL IS STILL GOING ON
(SEE LUKE 2:4–7)

In parts of the world like ours, you know, we can live the nativity scene for ourselves almost every day. Because we are actually living through the "drama of the land." Big companies buy up acres of land in the country's interior, and families that have lived there for years and years are then obliged to leave. When they arrive in the cities, Recife for instance, they look for somewhere to live. Often the wife is pregnant. They end up by building miserable hovels — you might say subhovels — where no one else wants to live, nearly always in the swamps. And there Christ is born. There is no ox or donkey, but there is a pig — pigs and chickens sometimes. That's the crib, the living crib.

At Christmas, naturally, I celebrate Mass in various churches. But I also like to say Mass in one of these living cribs. Why should I go on pilgrimage to Bethlehem, to the historic birthplace of Christ, when I see Christ being born here, physically, every moment of the day? He's called João, Francisco, Antonio, Sebastião, Severino.... But he is the Christ.

Oh, how blind we are, how deaf we are! How hard it is to grasp that the Gospel is still going on. — *TTG*, 14–15

In our part of the world the poor love dramatizations. These aren't shows or theatrical performances. It is the way children behave. When a child climbs on a chair and imitates an airplane, he actually is an airplane. He takes off. The engine roars. He flies through the clouds. He flies over deserts and seas. How dimwitted you would have to be not to see he really is an airplane.

One day I was walking back through a *favela*. A little boy came running along with his arms out wide. I nearly got in his way. I apologized: "So sorry! I didn't see your car coming." He looked at me with ineffable contempt: "My car? This is a spaceship!" He was navigating among the stars.

So when people here enact scenes from the Gospel, they aren't acting at all. They are really living these scenes. The Gospel is something alive. When Christ heals the blind, the deaf, the dumb, the paralytics, when he sets about resurrecting a child or an old friend, when he talks to the woman of Samaria, this is something very close to them.

It's the same with the crib. Instead of making a lovely artificial crib, they make a cradle out of an old packing case or an old gasoline can — as the poor do — and lay it down among the pigs. It sometimes happens, when mothers have to go out to work, that when they come home they find the pigs have eaten the baby. Naturally they do what they can to make a corner safe somewhere, but accidents will happen. Isn't that terrible?

This is how people find out what it was like for Christ to be born among the beasts. Children are still being born in the mud among the pigs today.   — *TTG*, 17–18

PRAYER

To the extent that we are conscious of the riches heaped on us, we have to do our utmost — and more — to serve, with all our heart and all our soul, as interpreters of nature and minstrels of God.

The Psalmist teaches us to lend our voices to the whole of creation and, in the wake of St. Francis of Assisi, we are urged to sing the praises of the creatures, including those that come from the Creator thanks to the collaboration of man, his "co-creator."

Without considering ourselves better than anyone else, but by making good use of the riches heaped on us by God, we are called:

- to present our sorrows and needs to the Lord in the hour of affliction, but equally to open ourselves to the joy of worshiping the Lord, happy in the knowledge that he exists and that he is God;

- to endeavor, permanently, to extend ourselves, to progress beyond selfishness, to enlarge our understanding, our forgiveness, our openness to love;

- to live, very concretely, the Lord's today in the place and the circumstances that he has chosen for us, and to strive, increasingly, to be pilgrims of the Absolute and citizens of the Eternal;

- to look at every human being, without asking what tongue he speaks or to what race and religion he belongs. The Christian can and must say to himself: "Now *there* is my brother or my sister," and he can and must add: "my blood brother or sister, since the same blood of Christ was shed for both of us, as indeed for all people."

This openness, this responsibility to God, is lived and realized in prayer, which brings us into direct contact with God and puts us through to him. Without prayer, there is no current, no Christian respiration.

Here I venture to bring in my personal experience of the role of prayer in human life. I was ordained a priest in my twenty-third year, in 1931. I was then living in Fortaleza, a small capital of North-East Brazil.

From that moment I understood that, in view of my decision to give myself unreservedly to God and my neighbor, it would be absolutely necessary for me to devote space and time to prayer, speaking and listening to God. Otherwise, in no time at all I would be depleted and have nothing to offer either my brothers or the Lord.

Knowing this to be true, I take advantage of a faculty that God has given me: that of waking up and falling asleep again at will. Consequently, I wake up every night at two in the morning and remain in prayer for two hours.

Of course, I am not suggesting that I am a great penitent. It is no sacrifice for me to "keep awake and pray." I have discovered that we are doing our soul an enormous injustice if we do not give it the opportunity to refuel itself, in the same way that sleep restores the strength of our body.

There are specific ways of refueling the mind and the spirit: contact with nature, music, conversation with friends and, for those who are blessed with faith, listening and speaking to the Lord.

So when I wake up at night, my first concern is to restore the unity within me. During the day, it is dispersed: my eyes and arms and legs go in all directions. At those privileged moments of the night, I endeavor to restore the unity of my being, that unity which, from the day of our baptism, is in Christ.

At those moments, a favorite prayer of Cardinal Newman often comes to my lips (here I am quoting it from memory and simply retaining its spirit): "Lord Jesus, do not remain so hidden in me! Look through my eyes, listen through my ears, speak through my lips, act with my hands, walk with my feet. May my poor human presence recall, at least remotely, your divine presence."

For when Christ and I are *one,* how delightful it is to speak to *our* Father in the name of all people, of all times and all places. The two of us having become *one,* we worship our Father (and I cherish in my memory all the most beautiful things my eyes have seen in my life), we give thanks to our Father, we ask his forgiveness (and I like to add: "As for me, Lord, I'm a qualified ambassador of human weakness, because all those sins of men, I too have committed, or could in the future"), and we present the petitions of our brothers.

In my petitionary prayer, I like to tell God of all the things that happened yesterday:

- I met that poor workman, unable to find a job. . . . I think of him, concretely. But beyond him, I think (we think) of all the unemployed in today's world.

- Then I encountered that young girl, just awakening to life. I think of her, but beyond her, I think of all the young, with their problems, their hopes, or their distress.

Obviously, I do not forget my breviary. And, always, the beauty and wealth of those moments come from unity with Christ.

This vigil devoted to prayer prepares me for the eucharistic celebration, the peak moment of the day. And, by the grace of God, the Eucharist envelops the whole day in wonder, because everything, in all simplicity, becomes offertory, consecration, communion.

Let me also convey to you at least the joy and the beauty of living communal prayer in our grassroots communities, which we call "basic church communities."

A baptism celebrated by one of our grassroots communities is quite different from a mere social and family event, which is sometimes reduced to seeking a godfather who will protect the child. With us, the whole church community is involved. The entire community prepares to celebrate the official incorporation of a new member into the church and the community, which is the living image of Mother Church.

The same is true of the other sacraments. It is not difficult to imagine the power and beauty of a communal confirmation, or again, of a wedding, a priestly ordination, and even an episcopal ordination, celebrated in this spirit.

To hold celebrations of this kind, a price has to be paid: they cannot be improvised or reduced to formalities. But when we behold true community celebrations, we really relive the early days of the church and come closer to the ideal that eluded us: to be one heart and one soul in Christ.

The Christian, according to his religious dimension, is the well-adjusted follower of Christ: one with Christ and made responsive in him and by him to the whole of human life. He is the Christian who is the universal brother of all and loves to give prayer its communal dimension, both visibly and within a group.

I have tried to express all this in the simple and humble words of the following prayer:

> How poor you will remain until you discover
> that you do not see best
> with open eyes.
>
> How naive you will remain until you learn
> that when your lips are closed, there are silences richer
> than torrents of words.
>
> How clumsy you will remain until you understand
> that joined hands can do far more than restless hands
> which may inflict
> the unintended wound.   — CRSA, 15–19

LIVING OUR PRAYER

I love hearing the apostles ask: "Lord, teach us how to pray." We may sometimes think we've learned how to pray already. All the same, knowing the Lord's Prayer by heart isn't enough. The important thing is to learn to live the prayer the Lord has taught us. Beginning with "Our Father." Are we really convinced that God is the Father of us all? Not merely "my" Father, but "our" Father. If he is "ours," then we are all brothers and sisters.

People with the same father are brothers and sisters. It's very easy at Mass to say, "Peace be with you," to the person standing next to you; but after that we each go home and the other person is forgotten. If the other people were really our brothers or sisters and we knew they were ill, destitute, perhaps even dying of hunger, we should do all we possibly could for them and more.

When I was in Rio de Janeiro, one day a man came to see me. He came from Fortaleza, the town where I was born and grew up. He hadn't been able to find a job. I tried to help him. I wrote to a friend of mine who owned a big shop: "Dear friend, see if you can take Antonio on. He's my brother, my blood-brother. He hasn't any work and he's hungry. Can you give my brother, my blood-brother Antonio, a job?"

My friend was on the telephone to me immediately: "Look, your brother Antonio's just arrived. I've given him a job. But, Dom Helder, how can your brother have possibly fallen into such poverty — your own brother?"

"Is he really with you already?"

"Yes, he is. And I've also given him some clothes and shoes since he was looking like a tramp. But I suspect you told me he's your brother so that I wouldn't be able to refuse."

"Not at all. He is my brother, I tell you."

"Brother, brother: I know, all the world's your brother!"

"Honestly, he is my brother. We've got the same Father."

"Didn't you tell me: blood-brother?"

"We call those blood-brothers who have the same blood of the same father in their veins. So there you are: Christ shed the same blood for you, for me, for Antonio. So we're brothers in the blood of Christ."

Yes, the Lord requires that, having prayed and, precisely because we have prayed, being filled with the Spirit of God, we turn our gaze on our human brothers and sisters.

Then again, when we say, "Thy will be done." It's easy enough to accept God's will when it coincides with our own. We know exactly how to ask the Lord for things, but the Lord had better look out and agree with what we want. And on no account should the Lord think or want anything different.

And yet, very often what we ask for isn't what is good for us. We are like little children, as far as the Lord is concerned. A father knows better than to give his child the knife the child wants to play with or to let the child go down the stairs on his own. You know the prayer I love to say? "Lord, may your grace help me to want what you want, to prefer what you prefer." For, honestly, what do we know? We ought to do everything as

though all depended on us, at the same time putting ourselves
into the Lord's hands, knowing that our own strength lies in
offering him our weaknesses.

We really need to learn to live Christ's prayer. To learn, for
instance, how to share our bread. When we pray, we know
we've got bread at home, not only for today but for the whole
month, perhaps for the whole year and even for the rest of our
lives. There wouldn't be any problems if, as well as ourselves
who have enough bread for the rest of our lives and even for
our heirs, there weren't our brothers and sisters who haven't
even got their daily bread and who endure hunger in desperate
poverty.

If only we Christians, charged with the terrible responsibility
of bearing the name of Christ, if only we could at least really
behave like brothers and sisters. I remember seeing a Franciscan going by one day and thinking, "How rash, how brave, to
bear the name of Francis of Assisi!" And we who are brave and
rash enough to bear the name of Christ, what about us who call
ourselves Christians? What a responsibility we have!

—TTG, 57–59

PROBLEMS FOR FAITH

There are some obscure passages in the Gospel. I think anyone
who claims to understand everything in holy scripture, as in life,
can't be altogether human.

For my part, I have a number of mysteries stored up in my
mind. When I reach the Father's house, I shall have several questions I want to ask the Lord. Not straightaway, since I shall be
overjoyed at seeing the Lord face to face and being with my
brothers and sisters. But later on, after a few days. Of course,
this is only a manner of speaking, since face to face with the
Lord all mysteries vanish — a way of saying that in our small
corner of planet Earth, this speck in the universe, we can't see
or understand everything.

The sufferings of the innocent for instance, above all those of little children. This is a constant problem, a mystery, to me. I say, "Lord, I don't pretend to understand you. Still less do I presume to judge you." But the problem doesn't go away. It will of course be resolved the moment I reach the Father's house. But I shall still feel like saying, "Father, I know you're a real father. But why, Father, do you build life on death?"

Talk about hyenas — we human beings are like hyenas ourselves, only somewhat more sophisticated. To keep ourselves alive, we kill cows, sheep, pigs. We live on the deaths not only of animals but of vegetables too. The whole chain of existence is made up of thousands of deaths.

I am archbishop of Olinda and Recife. For me to be here, someone had to die before I came — my predecessor. And it's always like this. There's only one case of life not being born from death, and that's the Holy Trinity; the Father, who for all eternity begets the Son; the Father and Son who together give life to the Spirit. This is Life, Life and only Life. But apart from the Creator and the angels, there is always the same terrible mystery: life that sustains itself on death.

This is a colossal question that human weakness can never hope to solve. But I can tell you, once I stand before the Lord, I shan't even have to ask it. —TTG, 64–65

NO MONOPOLY OF THE HOLY SPIRIT

Whenever the story of the centurion who had faith (Matt. 8:5–13) is read, I always wonder how there can be people silly enough to believe that only Catholics will be saved. As though the Holy Spirit were up there, singling out the Catholics or possibly the Christians, to breathe on them and only them.

No! Wherever in the world there are human creatures hungering and thirsting to love and help, trying to overcome self-centeredness, escaping from self; caring for their neighbors, listening to the voice of conscience, striving to do good, the Spirit of God is with them. I love the Lord's words: "Many will come from the East and from the West...." In the Father's house we shall meet Buddhists and Jews, Muslims and Protestants — even a few Catholics too, I dare say.

All too often we believe we have a monopoly of the truth. But the truth is so enormous. God, for instance. We live within God and we have God within us. But God is so great that, for us to comprehend — and comprehend means embrace — God completely, we should have to be even greater than God is.

I was very excited when the first photos were taken of the hitherto unknown, invisible side of the moon. What a surprise it will be when one day we see the Father face to face. Then we shall realize how poor, limited, and imperfect a vision of God we have now. And the same goes for truth. We have no monopoly of the Holy Spirit. We should be humble about people who, even if they have never heard the name of Jesus Christ, may well be more Christian than we are.   — TTG, 60–61

And you know the Holy Spirit doesn't have to wait for missionaries and bishops to transmit its message; it doesn't stop to choose the places where there are Catholics. They are everywhere, potentially: all people are the children of God, united through Christ. So the Holy Spirit breathes; and very often when the missionaries arrive they are really surprised to find that the Holy Spirit got there first!

It makes for some curious mixtures. We see it particularly in Brazil. We have many Africans in our country. We Christians imported slaves from Africa. They were brought here under appalling conditions. Even cattle were not transported like that. When they got here they were split up so that they wouldn't form groups: husbands separated from wives, children from parents. It was horrible! And as a recompense, as a first benefit of civilization, a first token of human and Christian advancement, they were baptized. Without any preparation, of course. That wasn't necessary: the baptism was enough in itself, wasn't it? All you needed was some water and the right words.... Nowadays we try to convert people before we baptize them. But in those days, when these poor creatures, these children of God, were oppressed and overburdened by our good intentions, I think the Holy Spirit protected them by letting them associate the names of our saints with their own gods and spirits.

For example, they often confuse the Blessed Virgin Mary with Iemanjá, the goddess of the sea. She is greatly honored in Brazil. And on December 8, when I see the enormous crowds that gather to celebrate the Immaculate Conception, I'm convinced that two-thirds of the people are probably thinking of Iemanjá. It's a real mixture of African religion and Christianity: they are there to honor the Blessed Virgin. They love the Mother of God, the Mother of Christ, sincerely; but they confuse her somewhat with the goddess of the sea.

When you're here in my house you often hear someone knocking at the front door and shouting: "Dom Helda! Dom Hebe!" All sorts of different names. It isn't the people's fault that my name is rather difficult to remember and pronounce! "Helder" is really quite difficult! But imagine if I were to open the door and say: "You've come to the wrong house. There's no one here called Dom Helda, or Dom Hebe!" People don't need to pronounce my name impeccably for me to know that it's me they're calling, it's me they're looking for. It's the same with the Mother of God, who is also the Mother of Men, and the Mother of Fishermen: it really doesn't matter if people confuse her name with that of Iemanjá!

You know, you have to start from where the people are. Imagine if I were to arrive among a tribe of Indians and say: "Right! Now we're going to speak Portuguese. Because Portuguese is a real language, rich in history and culture. I don't need to learn the poor language of the Indians. Only Portuguese." It's impossible. Incarnation means putting yourself on the level of the people you live and work with. Not so that you can stay there, of course, but so you can help them rise above it. The only way to help them rise is to start from where they are.

— *CB*, 122–23

THE UNITY OF CREATION

God has a weakness for human beings. God loves the whole creation but, in the creation, has an especially tender spot for us. This love between God and human beings is fantastic. Even if we hadn't sinned, I am convinced God would have found some good reason for becoming incarnate. He would have taken human nature, to teach us how to share in his divine nature.

It's wonderful what God did in creating human beings. We have much in common with minerals, with stones. We also have much in common with vegetables. Trees breathe, feed, grow; so do we. We are clearly brothers and sisters to the animals. Above us, we share in the nature of the angels and we also share in the nature of God. What an adventure, what a daring thing, to assemble so many differing characteristics in one creature! That's why we find it so hard to strike a balance: there are so many worlds tugging at us inside. It is Christ who gives us unity. Christ unites all those worlds that exist inside us.

I think it would be completely absurd to suppose that there is life only on earth, when there are millions and millions of other planets. When speaking of the Creator's preference for humanity, I'm only talking about our own little earth. I don't know what goes on elsewhere in the universe. But one day we shall know.

I remember when the first astronauts went to the moon, I ran into very simple people who refused to believe it. "It's United States propaganda," they said.

"No, it isn't. Not this time. Human beings have really got to the moon!"

"Why, then, it's an insult to God. We've really gone too far."

"No, we haven't, brother. Don't be alarmed. This is only the beginning of the beginning. It won't be long before we get to Saturn — and we shall get there — and then we shall see we haven't reached the end, the limits of the universe, but only the end of the beginning."

When I think of all those different worlds united in the human creature here on earth, I feel myself to be brother to each of them. Joyfully I lend my voice to the stones, the trees, the animals in my street and those in the forest. And I say: "Perhaps you don't know how to talk or think. Perhaps you don't know there's a Creator. So I shall speak for you. I'm lending you my voice."

By the same token I think that there are millions of creatures that perhaps have never heard the name of Christ, yet Christ is with them nonetheless. Christ is everywhere, with God's entire creation, and not merely with those who know him. The only difference between Christians who do know Christ and the others who don't is that we have greater responsibilities.

— *TTG*, 8–10

Human Beings Are Co-Creators

By virtue of a special covenant, willed by God, the Jewish people were chosen, among all the nations, to be a witnessing people, testifying above all to the oneness of God. It recognizes and proclaims one Lord and Master, a very holy God.

God the Creator of the world, in whom we believe, has always wished man to be his "co-creator." He has appointed man to tame nature and to complete his creation. Not content to know that man, like the whole of creation, is immersed in him, the Lord is everywhere, and it is in him that we breathe and act and find our being. Omnipresent by virtue of his creation, the Lord has established a very special and intimate covenant with man.

He wishes not only to give man being and life, but also to draw him into the very intimacy of his own life. With man he has made a new and definitive covenant.

In ancient days the Lord sent the witnessing people patriarchs and prophets, in order to sustain its faith in the one God. But in the fullness, the zenith of time, he sent his own Son, who took flesh by assuming, in the Virgin Mary, a human nature through the working of the Holy Spirit. God was made man in Jesus Christ.

By coming to us in this way, by living on our earth, Christ brought us a stupendous revelation. He revealed to us that God, the Almighty and the Most High, the Father of all people, wished us to become in Jesus Christ — the only begotten Son — sons by adoption, called to share in the very life of God.

Like his Father, who creates with us, God-made-Man, our Brother, wishes us to complete his work of redemption. He desires us to be "co-redeemers," so that liberation from sin and from the consequences of sin may be achieved in us and with us.

Lastly, the Holy Spirit — like the Father sharing his creation with us and the Son drawing us into his work of redemption — wishes us to collaborate in his permanent work of sanctification. He desires us to be, as it were, instruments of "co-sanctification."

To us human creatures falls the duty of responding to these divine initiatives, which are beyond our boldest dreams.

— CRSA, 14–15

EVERYONE HAS A VOCATION

When God our Father calls us to life, he chooses a human family into which we are to be born, a nation to which we are always linked during our time on earth, and, respecting our freedom, he establishes a plan of life for each of us. He has thought of us from all eternity. For him there is no future and no past, but only today, always the same and always new.

The Holy Spirit sees to it that we live up to the Father's plan as well as possible.

It is wrong to think that the Father only has a plan for the life of a few creatures. None of us, no matter how humble, is thrown into life without a direction to follow, without a precise way ahead, left merely to chance.

There is divine providence! Chance does not exist.

There are many people who pass through life without know-ing that divine providence has thought about each one of us, that providence has a plan that can be upset by us or by others.

Vocation is a call — a call of God to the different states of life and to different professions.

Vocation to the priesthood or to religious life certainly de-serves special care and the prayers of us all. This is not because priests and religious are more important or greater than others, but because of the role they play in the church and in humanity.

Yet have you ever thought about how great is the call to matrimony? Always remember that fathers and mothers are partners with God in bearing and bringing up their children.

Have you ever thought that for every honest profession there is a call from God?

I know a priest who likes to shake hands with the trash col-lectors when they are loading the refuse onto the truck. They try to clean their hands on their clothes. The priest, rightly, says: "No work stains human hands. What makes hands dirty is stealing, or greed, or the blood of our neighbors!"

But would you like to give Christ a special joy? Then work for an increase in religious and priestly vocations: let them be numerous and holy.

There are those who say they have never felt a vocation, in the sense of a call from God. But God certainly calls. Only those who create silence within themselves will hear ... the silence of hope, of generosity and of love.   —*SE*, 61–63

CONVERSION EVERY DAY

We are never completely converted. We have to keep on con-verting ourselves every day....

One day some nuns invited me to say Mass to mark the six-tieth year of profession of one of them, a very holy woman. Pretending not to be quite sure what anniversary it was that we were celebrating, I said to her, "Sister, let me get this straight. Exactly how many years have you spent in the religious life?"

Very humbly and first looking around to make sure there was no one else eavesdropping except God, she replied, "Honestly, Father, I've only spent one day in the religious life. Because every day I have to start all over again."

What a remarkable answer!

We human creatures bear within ourselves great riches and great weaknesses.

We are living temples, living churches. The Lord is within us, with the Holy Spirit. At catechism, we're taught the seven gifts of the Holy Spirit. Obviously the Holy Spirit isn't so stingy as to dispose of only seven gifts. We single out only the main ones. But the Holy Spirit has remarkable gifts for each of us. There is no one on whom the Holy Spirit doesn't bestow a tailor-made, personalized minimum of charisms.

But to offset these riches there is always self-centeredness too. So we also single out the seven principal manifestations of self-centeredness, the "deadly sins": envy, laziness, pride, impurity, avarice. . . . But there are many more than that. They are called "deadly" because each one of them gives rise to many other weaknesses.

God works this marvel: that even though he resides with us and in us, we still retain our weaknesses. It's up to us to avoid giving way to pride, to keep on the alert. We have to keep the process of conversion going all the time.

At the end of the Council, I was sitting next to the president of the Lutheran World Federation. He said, "Well, Dom Helder, we've had to wait hundreds of years before getting almost what Luther was wanting. What a wonderful thing it is to see the Roman Catholic Church undertaking its own reformation!" Then, very humbly, he added, "Perhaps we of the Reformed Church are too proud of being reformed, when what we really need is a new reformation." To which I replied, "All of us, friend, and all our churches too, constantly need reforming. Conversion ought to be going on every day, since self-centeredness is ever-living. They say it only dies a few hours after we ourselves are dead."   — TTG, 76–78

HOLINESS

Very often people — particularly poor people, humble people — imagine that you are better, more virtuous, than you really are, and want to canonize you, even while you are still alive. There is a story about St. Francis of Assisi that I am very fond of, and that I find helpful. One day Francis and Brother Leo were out walking together. Suddenly Brother Leo called out: "Brother Francis!" "Yes, I am Brother Francis." "Be careful, Brother Francis! People are saying remarkable things about you! Be careful!" And Francis of Assisi replied: "My friend, pray to the Lord that I may succeed in becoming what people think I am." It is a beautiful reply.

There is a danger of losing your head when simple people begin to think of you as an extraordinary man, as a saint. But there are fortunately ways of guarding against it. For example, when I am about to go out and face a huge audience that is applauding me and cheering me, I turn to Christ and say to him simply: "Lord, this is your triumphal entry into Jerusalem! I am just the little donkey you are riding on!" And it's true.

Holiness . . . Well, "Holy is the Lord." Holiness is the Lord. He is the only saint. There is only one Lord. But shared holiness is not a privilege reserved for exceptional individuals. It is a duty for all of us. Through baptism we all receive sanctifying grace, the grace that brings holiness. It is very naive to think that being holy means seeing visions, performing miracles, living a life that is very hard, very extraordinary! Being holy means living with sanctifying grace, living close to the Father, the Son, and the Holy Spirit, being one with your fellow human beings. And that is a duty for all of us.

There is no single definition of holiness: there are dozens, hundreds. But there is one that I am particularly fond of: being holy means getting up immediately every time you fall, with humility and joy. It doesn't mean never falling into sin. It means being able to say: "Yes, Lord, I have fallen a thousand times. But thanks to you I have got up again a thousand times." That's all. I like thinking about that.

When you are approaching death it is very tempting to count
your weaknesses and your failings and your sins, and perhaps
to lose courage. I think it is better not to count them at all,
not even to talk about them: "Yes! My weaknesses and my failings and my sins are innumerable, and very serious! But there is
something far greater than all my weaknesses and failings and
sins: the mercy of the Lord!"

Oh, I could tell you some wonderful things about the mercy
of the Lord!   —*TTG*, 36–37

HUMILITY

I feel — it is my personal conviction — that humility is truly
an essential virtue. Without true humility, we cannot advance a
single step in the spiritual life. But our heavenly Father is ac-
quainted with our weakness. He knows that we have pride and
self-respect. I am under the impression that God himself, our
heavenly Father, purposely sets in our path each day some four
or five small humiliations, and four or five big, first-class humiliations during our lifetime. I still remember the first great
humiliation in my life.

As I said, this happened when I was a seminarian. One day
I heard that a professor of psychology at the Normal School in
Fortaleza was teaching erroneous ideas: materialism, behavior-
ism. Today I know that she did not realize what she was doing,
poor benighted creature! She did not understand.

Well, this is what I did. I had been shown some of the notes
taken by this professor's students, and I showed them to our
rector.

"We must reply to this!" I said. "We must help the students!
We must make it known that a professor at the Normal School
is teaching materialistic enormities!"

With the approval of my rector and the professors I wrote
an article, under the pen name of Alceu da Silveira. It created a
sensation in the town — a small town where everyone read the
paper. And I was proud! My classmates read the article! I was

just beginning my studies in philosophy, had not yet received the tonsure.

The professor I had denounced replied and I replied in my turn — two, three, four, five times! This was polemics! I was convinced that the whole town was excited over the affair.

My archbishop was not there. But his vicar-general lived at the seminary, and he was one of those saints that God has ordained I should meet from time to time in my life. He sent for me, and I was absolutely sure it was to congratulate me on my writings. But here is what happened:

"Is it true that those articles really come from your pen?" he asked.

"Yes, Father, it is true," I answered, very touched, very satisfied.

"Then, my son, I must tell you that the article published in yesterday's paper is the last article you will write."

"Oh, Father! That's impossible! Excuse me, but have you read the enormities that woman wrote in today's paper? No, Father! At least let me reply to that last article of hers. I have already written it and can show it to you."

"The article that appeared yesterday is your last."

I went out, my mind in a whirl of stormy thoughts. For the devil is rather smart, and the devil was prompting me. "The vicar-general is a saint," he whispered, "but even a saint is influenced by the bonds of family and friendship!" For now I must tell you that this professor at the Normal School was the sister-in-law of the vicar-general. You can imagine his temptation! I was eighteen years old, and the storm I was swept up into was terrible.

Fortunately I passed the chapel, and entered it, since I had complete freedom at the seminary, with the protection of the rector, the professors, and my friendly classmates. As I found myself face to face with an image of the Blessed Virgin, I recall that I said to myself, "I shall leave here only when I have recovered my calm."

I am convinced that had I not managed to submit to the humiliation that had been sent me that day, not by the devil, but by the heavenly Father, I would very probably, no, surely, have abandoned the seminary and perhaps the faith as well.

I remained in the chapel one hour, two hours, two and a half hours. My comrades went out in great silence, going afterward to the refectory. They had heard the news, because the rector had been informed. And with the backing of the rector and some of the professors, they were planning a demonstration against the vicar-general.

But meanwhile I was in the chapel repeating, "Holy Mother, I will not leave this place until I have recovered my calm."

At the end of two and a half hours, I suddenly recalled that it was the feast day of St. Martha: July 29. And I recalled the words, "Martha, Martha, you worry and fret about so many things, and yet few are needed, indeed only one. It is Mary who has chosen the better part." And I immediately understood that what had seemed to me the defense of truth and faith had been pride. I was preparing for the tonsure in a state of pride!

This cured me. I made an act of contrition. But the devil was lying in wait for me: my colleagues staged a big demonstration on my behalf. "Continue!" they urged me. "You must continue!"

But I told them the whole story and recounted the revelation that had come to me.

"Please," I implored them, "help me to understand that it was pride."   — VP, 142–44

GROWING IN HUMILITY

Today there are those, probably many, who despise two important virtues: obedience and humility. Here I want to look at humility so that we can understand God's humility better, though obedience too has a special place in human life.

The truth is that those who despise humility do not know what it is. Far from being a virtue of slavery, humility is a synonym of truth, particularly truth about the virtues we have or think we have.

A person can try to grow in humility by seeking, truthfully, to see what qualities they have or have not, and in the case of having some good points, they can see how much is there naturally, how much has been given, how much has been acquired by effort. But after that, they should realize that every good thing in a human creature has come from God.

For humility is not false modesty. Intelligent persons, for example, should not pretend that they have no intelligence. Rather they should be aware that it is a gift from God and not think that they are as bright as if the sun shined in their heads, while others have brains full of breadcrumbs.

God neither forgets nor denies his infinite intelligence. The humility of God consists of living with human limitations and human meanness, just as a father adjusts his pace when walking with his small son who is not yet able to cope with long strides.

Why don't we study the grandeur and beauty of true humility?

— *SE*, 72–73

SIN AND SELF-RIGHTEOUSNESS

We have so exaggerated the problem of sin. We are such Pharisees. We stick the label "sinner" on other people as though we had no sins of our own.... Who can cast the first stone?

Sin isn't what other people say we've done. It's what our conscience tells us: "You've done wrong. You shouldn't behave like that."

I well remember a poor woman coming to see me. "Look, Dom Helder," she said, "my story's like many others you've heard already, I'm sure. My mother died. I was brought up by an aunt. One day, when I was with my boyfriend, he made me pregnant. My aunt very brutally threw me out. I ended up with those other women in the brothel quarter.

"Some kind-hearted women happened to notice that I was unhappy doing that kind of work, living that kind of life. They told me how I could tear myself away from it and bring up the three kids I had by then. They suggested I rent a little room. They even bought me a sewing-machine.

"You know, Dom Helder, I've done everything I could to satisfy the demands of the grand and beautiful ladies who order clothes from me. But their demands are never-ending. And when it comes to paying, they say, 'Come back on the first of the month!' Money's no problem for them.

"It's two and a half years now since I tore myself away from the brothel quarter. But since then, on seven or eight occasions, I've found myself without enough money to feed the kids; they've been crying with hunger. So once again I've had to go looking for men."

She realized that I was upset and trembling. But she went on, "I don't want to mislead you. I went out looking for men again seven or eight times because my kids were hungry, but three or four times too because the loneliness was so crushing."

Yes, believe me, the Lord understands what victims feel. The Lord isn't here to tote up our unfortunate sisters' sins. They are victims.

We churchmen frequently make too much of women's sins and sexual sins in general. As if sexual sins were graver than sins against compassion. Good heavens! How often we offend against compassion when, for instance, we inveigh against prostitutes.

We must keep the Gospel story of the adulterous woman ever in mind. I'm sure it would have been quite easy to find an adulterous man. There's no adulterous woman without an adulterous man. But it was less trouble to seize on the woman, drag her into the square, and pass judgment on her. And they were getting ready to stone her to death according to the law. To feel satisfaction, almost joy, at seeing the law enforced even on someone who's actually guilty, may well be a lack of charity.

Ought we to rate sexual sins as worse than sins against compassion?   — TTG, 72–74

We talk a lot about sins, but I am happier talking about weaknesses. We even talk of mortal sins. But the church teaches that, for there to be mortal sin, there must be grave matter, full awareness, and total consent. This means that even when the offense to God is grave, if consent is not total or if awareness is not full, it isn't a mortal sin.

Whenever you know people from the inside, you realize there's much more weakness than malignancy. And I know Christ loves repeating, "Father, forgive them, they don't know what they're doing." This is always my trust, my hope, when I hear of someone being written off as monstrous, perverse, beyond redemption.   — *TTG*, 33

I wish I could have been present to see this scene of the woman caught committing adultery (John 8:3–11). Especially when Christ was calmly writing on the ground. The bystanders must have been intrigued, possibly nervous: What was Jesus writing?

However, despite the warning Christ gave us then, we still go on carrying stones about with us. We always have stones ready for throwing at other people. It's a terrible thing, this mania of ours for passing judgment, judging and condemning. The process of conversion isn't easy....

And yet, reaching the state of not judging others anymore would be a notable way of avoiding being judged ourselves. For Christ has said, "Do not judge. You will be judged by the standard by which you have judged!"

If I don't judge, I shall have the magnificent surprise — when I reach the Lord's presence and nervously wonder, "My God, what's going to happen to me now?" — of hearing Christ say to me, "Don't worry, son. You've done your best not to judge. No judgment for you." Ah, that will be great!

It's difficult not to judge, not to condemn, not to put other people to death, those whom we think evil or dangerous. I'm thinking, for instance, of the battles that have to be fought against injustices and for more justice. The ideal thing would be not trying to defeat but to convince.

If I had been born into a rich family, a very rich one or even too rich a one, if I had never breathed any other atmosphere, if I had always traveled by car, never venturing into those districts where misery reigns, never hearing, never seeing, I'm sure my own reactions when people spoke to me about injustice would be the same as those I encounter among the rich, the very rich and particularly the too rich.

There are countries that still retain the death penalty. And it happens from time to time that someone is executed who turns out later to have been innocent. Mistakes will happen.

The same with prison: the time will come, I believe, when we shall be ashamed of having thought it quite normal to shut up our brothers and sisters in cages, like hyenas and wild beasts.

Of course society has to be protected against the wrongs a handful of people may commit against the common good. But it's increasingly possible now, given our advances in knowledge, to have recourse to psychology and education in preference to the barbarity of imprisonment and the death penalty.

— *TTG*, 97–98

Jesus says he is the gate, the gate of the sheepfold, of the corral (John 10:9–16). So why are we often tempted to be the gate ourselves? Besides the true gate — which is Christ — we also set ourselves up as a gate. Everyone's got to go through our gate, ours: our ideologies, our definitions, our ways of doing things. This won't do! Christ is enough. One gate is enough — Christ.

Christ also tells us he has other sheep. Elsewhere he relates how he leaves the ninety-nine that are well-behaved to go in search of the hundredth one, which has followed its own devices or perhaps a different shepherd.

Quite often I meet the ninety-nine sheep, frustrated and even furious because they think the shepherd has deserted them. Why should he bother about the hundredth one? It only had to be well-behaved and sensible like them!

We're like the prodigal son's elder brother. There's nothing at all uncommon about the jealousy displayed by those who have stayed faithful, who have never given offense, who have never grieved their parents. Here we are, faithful, loyal, where we belong, but full of pride. What? Our father is preparing a feast, a banquet for the good-for-nothing who's wasted the family fortune? How unfair! It is a terrible temptation to shut the shepherd up inside our sheepfold, behind our own gate.

— *TTG,* 101–2

One day I was with a mixed group of youngsters. They were talking very freely to me, in the idiom they use today. At one point one of them said, "You know, Dom Helder, I've been told the Gospel stories. But I've actually lived the story of the prodigal son [Luke 15:11–32], only in my case I lived it the other way round. It wasn't the son who ran off; it was my father, with another woman. Then my mother ran off, with another man. . . . That's life today, whether you like it or not. We children are the ones who've stayed at home."

He went on: "I once heard someone say the prodigal son in the Gospel must have already lost his mother or she would certainly have found some way of persuading him not to leave. But my story's not confined to me. It's a story that keeps on happening; other youngsters know it all too well. My father's living with the mother of one of my friends here now, so what are we to do about it? Deep inside, I want to protest, to rebel. But then I say to myself, 'No, it's not Christ's fault.' And if in the end I don't judge my father or mother, it's because Christ has taught me human understanding."

Dear friends, that day I read the parable of the prodigal son from a totally new angle. Through the eyes of the child of prodigal parents. It's easy enough to be understanding and kind when we've got everything we need. But what about when we haven't got anything, like this young lad?

There are times when understanding leads us into unlimited indulgence. Sometimes, however, to help our brothers and sisters, love requires us to take a tougher line.

I often come across fathers and mothers in a state of total bewilderment. They are torn between an old, insufficiently nourished, possibly dying love and the hope of new love. I can understand. But before saying, "I understand," I try to put up a struggle: "You've no right to do this. Think of your children.

Don't think only about yourselves." I try to rouse their sense of responsibility, to remind them of their duties and I urge them to make the necessary sacrifices. I fight. But eventually, if I'm not understood, it's I who have to understand. The last word, the last way of loving, has to be understanding.

Plainly, we can't be exactly like the Lord; we are only human creatures. But when I ponder how the Lord loves, I get the feeling that in every case it's different, depending on the individual.

I began thinking this when I was in the seminary. I was the librarian. I began by reading the books that appealed to me most, then those I was obliged to read, and finally the rest. Among the rest I spotted the writings and revelations of a number of saints. I read about two dozen of them. I then went to see the man who was much more to me than a professor of dogmatic theology. He was, you might say, my professor of life, professor of human understanding. "Look," I said, "I know what these various accounts say isn't the dogma of the church. I know these saints may have produced these revelations, these confidences ascribed to Christ, out of their own imagination. But I can't bring myself to think they are all made up. So why doesn't Christ say the same thing to each of them?"

My professor smiled: "My son, we can't measure God's infinite love with our petty human measures." And he went on to say these remarkable words, "God loves each man, each woman, in a uniquely individual way."

I was delighted by this, since it struck me that this was the way I loved too. How upset I used to get when I was little and people asked, "Who do you love most: Daddy or Mummy?" I loved my father as father and my mother as mother. Differently, but just as much.

It's hard to love like God, sharing one's love without dividing it, loving each individual without withdrawing any of one's love from the others. We're so grasping. We can love only by devouring. We feel we're being robbed if the person who claims to love us has eyes for others too.   — *TTG*, 111–13

When the Lord laid down this very strict law about the indissolubility of marriage (Matt. 19:3–9), he said in reply to the question about what Moses had commanded, "This was because you were so hard-hearted." I think our hard-heartedness needs honest and courageous examination.

The Lord walks with his people. He keeps us company. He listens to us. He assesses our weaknesses. Today, too, he understands the complexities and strains of the times. Personally, I am quite certain we churchmen ought to be Christ's living presence among his people; we ought to have the guts to ask ourselves in such complex times as these whether a more generous approach and understanding might not in certain cases be right and appropriate.

I know you may say, "But even today marriage is still a sacrament. Our Lord affords all the help required by the sacrament, of which both parties are the ministers." But, I insist, we shepherds ought to have the guts to see the difficulties as they are.

"But what about the children?" you object. I know. I come across many children of divorcees. I know the sort of dramas they have to live through. But when a couple reaches the point of tearing one another apart or of even coming to blows, this too is not the most helpful of scenarios for children to grow up in.

No, the whole problem needs to be reexamined. And Christ's words can help us to do it. He speaks of hard-heartedness. I think he understands and is inviting us to understand the strains and difficulties of our times.   — *TTG,* 116–17

The parable of the laborers in the vineyard (Matt. 20:1–16) certainly isn't meant to be a lesson in economics. In countries like mine that have large numbers of workers out of work, it's very tempting for employers to impose their own terms by playing off one against the other: "If you don't agree to my rates of pay, no problem! There are dozens, hundreds, outside only hoping for that." No, Christ's teaching taken as a whole shows the parable isn't a lesson in economics, but a lesson about the spiritual life: you can gain in one second what you haven't deserved over any number of years, possibly even over a lifetime.

The story makes me think of the man known as the "good thief." For him to have been on a cross, next to Christ, no doubt he had done some pretty terrible things in the course of his life. His mate, the one known as the "bad thief," kept hurling his taunts at Jesus: "If you've done such a lot of miracles, save yourself and take us with you." But the good thief had the honesty and humility to say, "You and I deserve to be here. But he doesn't. He's different from us, he's good. . . . Lord, remember me when you come into your kingdom." These few words were enough. The Lord didn't say, "Thank you for the kind thought. In a few years' time when you've atoned for your life, which hasn't been by any means exemplary, I'll admit you." No, he said, "This day you will be with me. This very day."

Isn't that fantastic! One second of good-will, of perfection, of grace received and lived, can be worth a whole lifetime.

This isn't easily grasped by people who have worked their guts out trying to live their entire lives according to the rules. Like in the parable about the prodigal son's elder brother, the Lord invites us, the "faithful ones," to understand the feelings of the shepherd who makes such a fuss over the sheep once lost, now found — to share his joy, instead of shutting ourselves away in rebellious envy.   — *TTG*, 122

The ideal, really, would be to hear the Lord say to me on the day of judgment: "You will not be judged, because you have refrained from judging others." As you know Christ said that we should be judged according to the standard we used for judging others. So if we refrain from judging, we even may not be judged ourselves. Sometimes I try to imagine Christ saying to me: "Now look here, you've taken this mercy business a bit too far: you've taken advantage of it." But that's impossible, because no one can go further than Christ in his mercy. He is mercy; he is understanding.

Oh, if only I could help — I can't do it, but the Lord can — to spread that understanding throughout the world. Understanding instead of judgment. Understanding doesn't always mean approval. But understanding instead of condemnation.

— *CB,* 217–18

CHRIST IN THE EUCHARIST AND CHRIST IN THE POOR

It was becoming clear to us that the eucharistic Christ cannot accept an excess of glorification while the other Eucharist — Christ living among the poor — is oppressed.

One day a delegation came to see me here in Recife. "Dom Helder, a thief has broken into one of our churches and opened the tabernacle. Obviously he was only interested in the ciborium, and he threw away the hosts — threw them down into the mud! Do you hear, Dom Helder, the living Christ thrown into the mud! We have rescued the hosts and carried them in procession back to the church, but now we must have a great ceremony of atonement." "Very well, I agree. We will organize a eucharistic procession. We'll invite the whole diocese. And it really will be an act of atonement."

On the day of the ceremony, when everyone was assembled, I said: "Lord, in the name of my brother the thief, I ask Thy pardon. He didn't know what he was doing. He didn't know Thou art truly present and living in the Eucharist. We are deeply shocked by what he did. But, my friends, my brothers, how blind we all are! We are shocked because our brother, this poor thief, threw the eucharistic Christ into the mud. But here in the North-East Christ lives in the mud all the time! We must open our eyes!" And I said that the best possible outcome of our communion with the Body of Christ in the Eucharist would be if Christ thus received would open our eyes and help us to recognize the Eucharist of the poor, the oppressed, the suffering. It was on this that we would be judged on the last day.

In Bogotá I was already aware of all of this. But the Eucharistic Congress was again very "triumphal." I don't blame my brother bishops of Colombia: their attitude was the same as mine had been a few years earlier.

After the International Eucharistic Congress in Bogotá there was an assembly of the bishops of Latin America in Medellín. And there we undertook a radical revision of the concept of eucharistic congresses. It is still important that we human beings work to glorify the Lord. But what can we do? We can't make God any more God-like, any more powerful or glorious. We are miserable creatures! But we can help our fellow men, and help the poor. "I was hungry, I was thirsty, I was in prison. . . . " We can glorify charity; charity is God. But we must go beyond the surface of the words: it isn't enough to distribute food and medicine and money. Every century has its own particular way of seeing and enacting charity, according to the needs of the time. In our time charity is helping to make justice triumph.

We were blessed with the opportunity of holding a national eucharistic congress here in Brazil, at Manaus, in 1975. The bishops, priests, nuns, laity, all of God's people who took part helped to make the connection between the sacramental Eucharist and the Eucharist of the poor: appearance of poverty, real presence of Christ. At the most solemn moment of the Congress an unemployed worker, an abandoned wife with her children, and a prostitute spoke to us all. It was very moving.

—CB, 156–57

THE BREAD OF HEAVEN
AND DAILY BREAD

I find it very moving to see the Lord so sensitive to people's needs. He has eyes to see they are hungry. He has ears to hear the clamor of his people. As his followers, we have no right to say: "Our job's to proclaim the Word, but it isn't our business to worry over food. Our food is the Bread of Heaven."

No. We're not shepherds merely of souls. We're shepherds of human beings, souls and bodies — with everything that involves. And today I am more than ever convinced the Lord is demanding of us that we go even further.

If there are people who are hungry, we should busy ourselves about hunger. It isn't the moment for discussing neat theories, discussing, for instance, whether this is or isn't paternalism. We ought straightaway to start doing whatever is possible, and a bit of the impossible besides. Particularly these days, when we are aware of the scandal of having two-thirds of the human race suffering from hunger and foundering in misery.

And since this hunger, this misery, stems from injustices and unjust structures, the Lord demands of us that we denounce the injustices. This is part of proclaiming the Word.

Denunciation of injustice is an absolutely essential chapter in the proclamation of the Gospel. And not merely a duty for the few. It is a human duty for everyone, a Christian duty for all Christians, and an absolute duty for the shepherds.

When some people read the accounts of the multiplying of the loaves, they imagine the Lord only intended to prefigure the Eucharist. So they go to Holy Communion. But, Lord, it seems clear enough to me that the very Eucharist itself ought to open our eyes to the misery and hunger of our fellow-beings.

Take the splendid history of the international eucharistic congresses. Originally, the primary purpose was to glorify the Lord hidden in the Eucharist. More recently, we have come to realize that Christ, "the bread of life," "the shared loaf," is insisting we should turn our attention to the multitudes hungering for friendship, love, understanding, justice, peace, bread.

So we must open our eyes. We must find a way not only of distributing the bread but of multiplying it.

Today Christ tells us it isn't enough to distribute bread to those who haven't got any. The essential thing is to work toward the creation of a more just world, in which there will no longer be a minority owning too much, among such multitudes of hungry people.   — *TTG*, 87–88

PRAYER AND ACTION

It's tempting to contrast Mary with Martha (Luke 10:38–42), contemplation with action, prayer with service. But you can't isolate one passage in the Gospel and forget the others: the story of the Good Samaritan, for instance. And still less that the Lord summed up the Law and the Prophets in two equally positive commandments: "Love God. Love your neighbor." So what I'm saying is, the ideal thing is to have Martha's hands and Mary's heart.

It's hard to understand how some women — and some men too — can devote their lives to prayer and nothing but prayer, when there are so many things to be done for other people. If God is truly God and truly Father, does he need our prayers? Certainly not because, if we prayed to him less, he would be less God, less powerful, less Father, less good, less perfect.

No. We're the ones who need to pray to God. Since, if we don't immerse ourselves in the Lord, we forget about our neighbor and then become inhuman ourselves.

I love contemplative religious. They pray on behalf of those who don't know how to pray, who haven't the time or think they haven't the time to pray, and even on behalf of those who don't want to pray because they don't know the Lord. Oh, if only they knew the Lord, they'd be the first to be praying!

I often think if there's any hope for the world — and there really is — we owe it to all these men and women praying in solitude on behalf of the rest of us.

True, there are self-centered solitudes. I'm not talking about them. I'm thinking of peopled solitudes. I like often to visit contemplatives. I make a point of bringing them up-to-date on the world situation: "You mustn't present yourselves alone before the Lord. You've got to carry the whole world in your hands, on your backs."

I like visiting panoramic viewpoints. When high above some town, from a skyscraper perhaps, I love looking down on the roofs of the houses. Under each roof are joys or suffering or anguish: "Lord, on behalf of those who are happy and those who are crushed...."

I love a peopled solitude. Peopled by the Lord, peopled by everyone on earth.   — *TTG*, 106–7

LAZARUS AND LIBERATION
(SEE LUKE 16:19–31)

When I listen to this parable I realize that Lazarus today is the entire "third world" sitting there at the rich world's gate — that world of countries growing richer and richer. There the "third world" sits, with its sores, its misery, its hunger.

We think the rich man in the Gospel ought to have invited Lazarus in to a meal: "Lazarus, Lazarus, come in! There's a chair for you among the guests. You can eat. We can talk. Speak up, Lazarus, say something." But, in my experience, when we talk to poor people like that, they still persist in looking on us as masters: "Yes, boss, yes, boss." "Son, I'm not your boss; I'm not your master."

"Yes, boss."

It's no easy matter to free the poor from their condition of beggary. The outstretched hand is almost a conditioned reflex. At a good suit, a kind face, a decent house, a nice voice, out comes the hand. Much needs to be done if we are ever to change the begging syndrome without pushing the poor into hating us, for this would only be to encourage the oppressed of today to become the oppressors of tomorrow.

What we've got to achieve is a world without oppressed or oppressors, but this can't be done by inviting the poor man out there at the gate to sit down at the rich man's table and then confronting him with dishes he never imagined existed and wines beyond his ken.

In Latin America, for the last century and a half, we have experienced political independence without economic independence. So we are well placed to warn our brothers and sisters in

Africa and Asia: "Look out! Those nations that are too powerful, the United States, Russia, China, are bound to have ulterior
motives. They help but, in giving, impose their influence. Colonialism will be reborn, brothers. In a different form, but it will
be colonialism just the same."

My dream for our Latin America and for the other continents being crushed, is a genuine economic integration without
external or internal colonialism either of left or right. Allowing
Lazarus to talk to the rich man, man to man, as human creature
to human creature, as child of God to child of God. Allowing
true dialogue, true sharing, in a world without domination.

—*TTG*, 115

MONEY

What Jesus tells us about money is very serious, very grave.

Money in itself we regard as morally indifferent, neutral.
With money one can do either good or evil. Even so, money can
change us. We think we own it, but it can very easily own us.

Good heavens! Once people start trying to make a profit,
they lose all sense of moderation. They keep on wanting more.

And yet, in the most critical of moments, money cannot be
a faithful friend. It's often my lot to be present when poor
people are dying and when rich people are dying. The poor have
their worries, their sufferings. They imagine that, if they had
money, they could call in the doctor and buy medicines. The
rich have everything. They're surrounded with medical experts
summoned from far away, who consult one another, deliver
their opinions, prescribe treatments and install extremely ex-
pensive equipment. But once the hour of death arrives, all this
is instantly useless, totally useless.

At the cemetery, the poor often don't even have coffins. They
are laid directly in the ground. The rich have coffins, family
vaults, wreaths. But for rich and poor alike, once below ground,
the dialogue with the worms is the same. And the dialogue with
the worms is the least of it. If we truly believe in eternal life, we

know the only thing we take with us is the good we have done during our lives.

Often people spend their lives, at the cost of great self-sacrifice, struggling to make money for the sake of their children. But when death draws near, it isn't hard to imagine the arguments breaking out among these children over the inventory and will. I've known the most united of families quarrel and split into factions at a death if there's any money about.

And many, many women whose husbands devote their lives to money-making come to me and say, "Dom Helder, I'd rather a thousand times not have the luxuries we've got and still have my husband's love. I've got everything you can imagine, but the most important thing of all is missing. I need my husband's love. And I'm losing that the faster the money rolls in."

—*TTG*, 120

During the Second Vatican Council, much was said about "a church serving and poor." This was essentially concerned with the church in relation to money and with its external signs of wealth. More serious however than the temptation posed by money is the one presented by prestige and power.

Sad to say, we have forgotten Christ's words: "I didn't come to be served but to serve." A church serving and poor...It's easy enough to call ourselves — as the Holy Father does — the servant of God's servants. But have we opted, once and for all, to serve? I say again: the temptation of prestige and power is strong, very strong.

A church serving and poor. A church that is servant of the poor. Opting for the poor doesn't mean spurning the rich. We have no right to spurn, not even to forget about, anybody. Why then this preference for the poor? The rich often consider they don't need us. In a brotherly way and without judging, still less condemning them, we ought to help them open their eyes, their ears, their consciences. But they make no demands on us. The poor, the oppressed, on the other hand, really do need us — cost us what that may.

Serving and poor, servant of the poor. I never get tired of repeating this: to do justice is the greatest love in our deplorably
unjust times. And the greatest poverty for the church is to consent to be misjudged, to risk its reputation, to lose its prestige.
To be treated as subversives, revolutionaries, communists perhaps: that's our poverty, the poverty Jesus asks of his church in
the age we're living in now.   — *TTG, 123–24*

PLEASURE

It's great to see Christ attending a party with his disciples and
Mary his mother. So many people with the best of intentions
have the idea that Christians and the party spirit don't go
together.

Anyhow, here's Christ attending a party. The Gospel doesn't
say whether there was dancing, but I'm sure there was. And
Christ didn't want the party to be a failure. He could have
turned the wine into water when the party started. But no, he
turned the water into wine just was as it was finishing. And he
did it because Our Lady asked him to.

Of course, it isn't a good thing to get drunk, to lose one's
senses. But who says drinking a little wine is a sin? I have the
deepest respect for those Christian communities who abstain
from the least drop of wine and alcohol. But in all brotherli-
ness I would remind them that Jesus performed his first miracle
by changing water into wine. More important still, when he decided to remain with us through the Sacrament of the Table, he
chose bread and wine. Wine, brothers and sisters!

When I was a little boy, we had a woman neighbor who was
very good but very strict. One day when I was making a lot
of noise, since I behaved like any other normal, healthy child,
this neighbor of ours grabbed me by the arm: "Little boy, stop
jumping about like that! The Child Jesus never used to jump
about. Stop shouting! The Child Jesus never used to shout. In
heaven, children keep quiet and sit still with their arms folded,
looking at the Lord."

Luckily for me, I already knew that this sort of vision of heaven was quite impossible. Heaven — ah me! — is quite different from that.   —TTG, 36–37

DEATH

There comes a time when one has to find the courage, and even the happiness, to prepare to reach the final destination, to join the Father.

God does things in a very intelligent, very delicate way. Next to the blessing of a holy death, the greatest blessing is a kind old age. A kind old age means growing old on the outside without growing old inside. One by one, signs appear pointing to the final destination. You no longer have as much energy. You have difficulty in seeing, or hearing. As a matter of fact, all my faculties are still functioning and I can still cope with my marathon trips abroad. But my heart tells me that the time has come to prepare to reach the final destination.

I think it is important to bear witness by really living one's death as the beginning of true life.

Of course I don't know how much longer the Lord is going to let me live. I'm not preoccupied with death. My motto, the motto of my life and my episcopacy, is *In manus tuas*, "Into Thy Hands." The Lord protects me so well that I can deliver myself with absolute trust into his fatherly hands. But I do still ask myself: "How will my sister death come to me?" What I find most difficult to accept, but I do accept it, is the possibility that the Lord may choose to let me survive myself, I mean, to let my body survive my mind. When I first went to Rio de Janeiro people still talked about Cardinal Arcoverde, the first Brazilian and Latin American cardinal. He had been a great bishop, but at the end of his life he became a child again, you know....It isn't easy to accept the idea of surviving like that. But I do accept in advance even that form of death.

I continue with my work: but all the time I am quietly and calmly preparing to receive the death the Lord intends for me.

— CB, 215–16

RESURRECTION OF THE BODY

First of all I should like to tell you about my reactions when very close friends of mine express grave doubts about the afterlife or maintain that death is the end of everything.

I don't enjoy and am not good at arguing. But I am utterly convinced that human beings have hungers and thirsts that can never be completely appeased here on earth. Hunger for truth, hunger for beauty, hunger for goodness, for the absolute, for the infinite, for the eternal. We aren't earthworms. When I am on the beach and see the waves rising, breaking, and vanishing back into the sea, I feel, I know, that we aren't waves. I don't know how to prove this. When I was studying philosophy, I was taught the five ways of demonstrating the existence of God. I didn't catch on very well: why did anyone need to demonstrate God's existence? It seemed transparently obvious to me that the Lord is there. It seems to me equally obvious that we are designed for eternity.

People wonder how the resurrection can be possible. How will it happen? Will an angel really sound a trumpet in the graveyards?

I've never had any problem over the resurrection. I say, "Look, friend, this body, your body now, the one I'm looking at, isn't the body you had in your cradle, it isn't the one your school friends used to know, it isn't the one that went to university. How many times has your body changed already, or will again completely change in the future? But you are always the same person. Since, inside your various bodies, there is one absolutely personal, unifying factor."

Or again I say, "Here's a piece of fruit." You eat half and the fruit becomes you. I eat the other half and the same fruit becomes me. The same fruit.

I realize these arguments aren't particularly good ones. But this is my way of stating my conviction that, within us, we each have a living spirit. When death comes, this living spirit survives.

And one day, when the Lord sees fit, this living spirit will retake shape, retake body, in some way we cannot imagine, any more than a newborn child can imagine the kind of body it will have at twenty. But we shall recognize one another. Eternity would be unacceptable, unnatural, if, having known and recognized and loved one another on this earth, we weren't to know and recognize and love one another on the new earth, in the new heaven. — *TTG*, 134

4

The Unity of Creation

"For me," Dom Helder told José de Broucker, "the transition from the natural to the supernatural, from reality to dream, is almost imperceptible." This description applies most of all to his "meditations," the reflections, prayers, and poems produced during his vigils between 2:00 and 5:00 in the morning. But in his everyday life, too, he constantly displayed an enchantment with nature, an awareness of animals and plants as living beings, part of a single Creation that is the expression of the love of the Creator and Father.

Some of Dom Helder's writings express the fear that human beings can destroy God's world, in particular through nuclear weapons: he was writing in the age in which there were two great powers that coexisted on the basis of "mutually assured destruction." Dom Helder belongs to a generation prior to the recognition of global warming; in fact, his attitude toward scientific and technological advance is extremely positive, and he frequently criticizes the idea that scientific discoveries lead human beings to usurp God's power. His underlying premise is that the loving Creator wanted human beings to excel and to share God's creative role. Dom Helder frequently refers to the idea that human beings are "co-creators." In Dom Helder's view what threatens the world is not human knowledge, but human selfishness.

Dom Helder says that he was a disciple of Teilhard de Chardin before ever reading his work; in other words, that his *ideas about human progress derive from a spirituality developed earlier in his life, probably in his childhood. Dom Helder was a devotee of St. Francis of Assisi, and some of the poems included in this chapter are modeled on themes of St. Francis. If Dom Helder was attracted by the idea of the "cosmic Christ," he owes it to a much earlier Christian notion, from the Pauline tradition. The fact that he expressed his vision for the future in the form of a "Mass for the Century" derives from a view of the Mass, in the words of his friend Zildo Rocha, "as a cosmic and universal act in which Christ, the Priest of Creation, gathers together and brings to perfection in himself all things, and takes them back, in the Spirit, to the Father."*

CO-CREATOR

Oh, if only we'd been able to understand and interpret religious events, and the living presence of Christ, to communicate to children, and young people, and adults, rich and poor alike, the terrific strength that can come from true religion. Think for instance of the Trinity and the wonderful story of the Creation: the Father who wants man to be co-creator with him; the Son who began the great work of liberation and wants man to be his co-redeemer; and the Holy Spirit who calls for and requires our collaboration. I think that is true religion. If we had been able to communicate it through religious instruction, through the catechism, we could have changed many things.

— *CB*, 97

I personally believe that the Lord has entrusted us with the task of subduing nature and completing the process of creation. That's why he has made us intelligent and creative. So I am not afraid of progress; I am not afraid of technology. What I won't accept is that technological progress should bring benefits only to a small privileged group that's growing smaller all the time. What I hope for is the socialization of technological progress, in the service of all mankind.

I'm a disciple of Teilhard de Chardin, totally and absolutely.
I think I was a disciple even before I read him. Through in-
spiration. When the Lord breathes a thought into the world, it
germinates here and there, apparently without communication.

But really I rely a great deal on Teilhard. We have the same
utopia; we are going in the same direction. Like him I believe
that humanity is moving toward a higher level of consciousness. In every race, every religion, every human group, there are
minorities that in the West I call "Abrahamic" — and that I'd
find another name for if I went to the East — minorities that
are very different from one another but have as a common de-
nominator the same hunger and thirst for a world that is freer,
more just, more brotherly: and when I see the vitality of all
these groups, I have enormous confidence in the future!

— *CB,* 99–100

A crisis of faith happens only when we are afraid and say:
"Watch out! Man is going too far! He is trespassing in God's
domain. Look: soon he'll want to be able to create life, and conquer death! He has already gone so far as to modify the human
brain, make the human heart beat artificially and violate space!
God cannot permit it: these powers belong only to him!"

But I can't imagine that God is jealous. Jealousy seems to me
a sign of deficiency: you are jealous when you want something
you haven't got. Well, I should feel very sorry for God if he had
to be jealous of man! We must keep going. We've hardly begun
to respond to the Lord's invitation to participate in nature, and
in his creative power. Why should we be afraid?   — *CB,* 170

Oh, how generous the earth is! We trample on her all through
our lives and yet she forever opens to feed us. And one day, like
a mother, she will open to receive us into her womb while we
await our resurrection.   — *TTG,* 150

KING'S SON

Lord,
isn't your creation wasteful?
Fruits never equal
the seedlings' abundance.
Springs scatter water.
The sun gives out
enormous light.
May your bounty teach me
greatness of heart.
May your magnificence
stop me being mean.
Seeing you a prodigal
and open-handed giver,
let me give unstintingly,
like a king's son,
like God's own.

— *DF,* 19

One morning, as I was leaving, I saw that the ants had eaten the leaves of my rosebush. That was serious! I bent down, picked up an ant, and holding it in my hand I looked it directly in the eyes and talked severely to it: "Why are you eating my rosebush? I insist: why are you eating my rosebush?" Then the ant gave me a lesson. Trembling all over, it looked at me and replied: "Why should you be the only one who has the right to enjoy the rosebush?" Yes, that was a lesson!

I'm the one that shows up badly in this affair. I said to the ant, "Why didn't you eat all this grass, here, instead of my rosebush?" And the ant did not reply. But next day when I went through the garden I noticed that the grass was not looking at me. And I said to myself, "Tsk, tsk, Dom Helder! What did you say?"

Why cannot the rosebush, the ants, the grass, and mankind share life with each other instead of warring to the death? It poses problems. God the Father, in his goodness, had to base life on death. We call certain animals hyenas because they eat carrion, that is to say, corpses. But we are doing the same, aren't we? Meat, fish? We merely clothe them in agreeable colors. Life always supposes death on every level. For me to be here in Recife, another archbishop had to die. It is a mystery. Life, life only without death, life springing from life and not from death — that exists only in the Holy Trinity. But afterward, when God wants to make something and scatter his riches about a little, he must be satisfied to create incomplete, unfinished, weak creatures. It is a great mystery.   — VP, 14

GOD KNEW
WITHOUT A SHADOW OF DOUBT

God knew it would have been impossible to create another God: another Infinite Wisdom, another Infinite Sanctity, another Infinite Creative Power....

In creating he would, necessarily, be creating the imperfect, the finite, the limited. With a humility that moves us to the very depths, and with an audacity that could come only from God, he created!

What humility, for Supreme Perfection to create the imperfect!

The Artist

Every artist hopes one day to reach perfection. When a new work is begun — a new creation in music, literature, painting, or sculpture — the artist is convinced that this time perfection will be attained. But as the work develops, the doubts start to come.

The Co-Creator Went Mad

The co-creator has created bombs — nuclear bombs, chemical weapons, biological warfare — which has brought him to the blasphemous position of facing the Creator saying: "I have the power to liquidate life on our planet, indeed, I could destroy the earth (which has had the privilege of the redemptive incarnation of your divine Son) more than thirty times over."

It is a matter of urgency to promote serious and profound studies in ecology.   —*SE*, 20

WE ARE IN GOD'S THOUGHTS THROUGH ALL ETERNITY

In God there is no succession of yesterday, today, or tomorrow.

In him there is only *today*, always the same and always new.

In God there is no routine, no repetition. How tiring sameness is!

We have been called to life by God. And because in God there is only a perennial today, let's constantly keep this thought in our minds: always the same and always new!

If we had not been called to life, no one could have asked anything for us because we would not even have had a name of our own. . . . This should be enough to drive us to an attitude of authentic humility. Pride is simply a lack of intelligence.

It was not only the saints and the prophets who were in God's thoughts through all eternity. . . . It was not only the kings and the wise and great men of this world: the most neglected creatures, the people who live in subhuman conditions of misery and hunger are sons and daughters of God, called to life by the Creator.

God does not accept praise, gifts, and honors from those who have no eye or heart for the human family, his sons and daughters of all races, all colors, all languages and creeds.

No one was created to be a slave or a beggar.

—*SE*, 21–22

WE ARE THE INTERPRETERS OF CREATION AND SINGERS OF GOD'S PRAISE

The psalms teach us to lend our voice to all creatures: to the mountains and the waters; to the trees and the birds; to the light that comes from above and to the earth that provides for us; to the creatures of the sea, from the tiniest fish to the whale.

Who has seen the same dawn twice? Who has seen the same sunset twice?

It is a pity that there are people who will go through life never having thought of watching the sunrise! Or without thanking our dear friend at nightfall!

Ah, but would you like to have seen the splendor of the act of creation? Then just think, creation is made anew, instant by instant, at God's hands.   — SE, 23–24

GOD'S DAZZLING ANSWER

In creating, God revealed an enormous preference for human beings. In us he summed up several worlds.

The minerals are our kin: we each occupy space and we are sensitive to the law of attraction.

The plants are our kin: like them we are born, we are nourished, we grow and we die.

The animals are our kin: sometimes we are surprised at the awakening of the animal within us.

The angels are our kin: our body is the bearer of a spirit and is kin to the heavenly spirits.

We share in the very nature of God, in his intelligence and in his creative power.

We have been raised to the glory and the responsibility of co-creators.

We have characteristics that are specifically human, like our unmistakable way of smiling.

Yet man and woman felt themselves so great that they gave in to the temptation of imagining that they were just one step away from becoming God.

And the Creator could have crushed the human creature; he could have completely suppressed the human race on earth.

But on the contrary, God's answer was dazzling, divine.

The Son of God, without losing his divinity, became incarnate, that is to say, he received a body like ours and a spirit like ours in the most pure womb of Mary, through the work of the Holy Spirit.

The man-God passed through the earth doing good. He brought us a divine message. He created a church to support us in our journey on earth. Above all he suffered and died for our sins!

This is what it means to repay evil with goodness. This is the divine answer to our ingratitude and our pride.   —*SE,* 30–32

EARTH, SISTER EARTH

Teach us
to continue the creation
to help the seeds
to multiply,
giving food
for the people
and for the beasts.

Teach us
to further the joy
you never tire of offering
when weary travelers find you,
a signpost to their home.

Teach us
to make the horizon
become a beautiful image
of creation's grandeur.

Teach us
to accept
the mediation of those
who wish to unite us
to our fellows,
as you accept the gift
of the water that binds
land to land,
no matter how great
the distances!

What do you suffer
in the dust of deserts?
How do you look upon
those of us who,
though capable of transforming
the waste to lushness,
prefer to be creators
of barrenness?

And how do you rejoice
in the rain
that brings forth your fruits?
And what pain do you feel
at the storms
that drown you with floods,
destroying plantations,
crushing houses and the lives
of animals, of plants, of people?
How great is the lesson
you give us,

O Earth,
more than sister:
our mother Earth!
All our lives
we walk carelessly across you,
and when life leaves us,

with no shadow of resentment,
you open up to us
your maternal bosom
to keep
our flesh,
our ashes,
for the joy
of the resurrection.

—*SE*, 83–86

BROTHER FIRE

Are you aware
of your beauty?
are you aware
of the artless grace
with which you fulfill
your high task
to conquer the dark?

Who taught
your flames to leap,
O dancer's envy,
light of step,
spinning in long pirouettes
none can forget?

Often you have the pain
to offer human life
as a sacrifice through
your touch of flame.

How do you find the courage
at such times, as you rise
in impetuous strength,
to give battle to the water;

and what are your thoughts
of the humble-noble firefighter?

With simplicity
you feed
the wood stove
and prepare the modest meals
of the families of the poor.

Do you not tremble with horror
when they speak of you
as a sign of punishment?
Yet with what great respect
do you consume and transfigure
the bodies of the martyrs!
Thank you, brother Fire,
for the warmth you bring
to freezing bodies
which have only you
as their help and salvation.

Thank you, brother Fire
for teaching us
to have a warm heart,
and helping us avoid
the emptiness of
a heart cold as stone.
Thank you, brother Fire
for the song in your flames
when, overcoming the darkness,
you become praise most pure
For our Father and Creator.

— *SE*, 87–89

WATER, MY SISTER WATER

When you were created
did you yet know
how many would be
the things you must do,
from the most noble
and beautiful
to the most base
and desolate?

Yes, you are beautiful
in the stillness of lakes,
in the flowing of rivers
(as humble brooks
or as the rushing of rapids),
in glittering cascades,
in the oceans that leave in us
the lingering images of
the Infinite.

Yet for those who have eyes to see
and ears to hear,
you are still more beautiful
as you labor, with joy,
on your round of lowly tasks:
the washing of clothes,
the cleaning of floors,
the quenching of imperious thirst.

And impressive are you
in your ceaseless travel,
lifted from the earth to the clouds,
and coming down again from heaven,
to bring life
to the plants,
to the animals,
life to the human race.

How did you receive
the dreadful commission
to bring the flood
and storms at sea
and wild lashing of the tempest?

Do you know
you give the chance
of heaven as the reward
of those who offer you
to quench the thirst
of their brother or sister?

Do you know
the sins of the human race
are to blame
for the many pains
you are forced to cure?
Thank you, sister Water.
Forgive
us who make you
perform cruel tasks.

Thank you,
above all
because you help us
to praise
the Creator and Father.

                              —*SE*, 90–92

BROTHER BIRDS

Do you think much
of the beauty of your plumes,
the enchantment of your song,
the grace of your flight?
Are you free

from pride and vanity,
or must you too
defend yourselves from
these failings that
humiliate us so much?

What joy you must feel
at the first flutterings of
your little fledglings,
and how you must remember
their first attempts to sing.

You surely must have thrilled
at soaring up, up in the air,
and racing to the horizon —
flying, flying, flying,
until you drop with exhaustion,
with the ripeness of emotion.

What do you suffer
when you are locked in cages;
how can you sing
when you still have wings
to prove you were born
for freedom?

What do you think
of a human voice in its beauty?
Is it anywhere near
the sweetness of your song?

When one of you dies,
is there sorrow?
Or do you believe
that you too
will one day rise up again?

Lord, in the name of those
who have no voice for singing
I offer you

the most beautiful songs
of your birds
and I ask of you
that we
may feel ashamed
of creating prisons for them.

Prisons for those
who received from you
the mission to fly.
Let us be ashamed
of listening to the singing
of caged birds,
when a song needs freedom more
than it does wings!
                              —SE, 93–96

BROTHER AIR

Have you noticed
how we humans
for all our civilization
transform you,
the guarantor of life
into a spreader of poisons?
Have you noticed
how we humans,
gifted with intelligence and reason,
are wounding nature
and preparing disasters
for ourselves
with our own hands?

How do you feel
when a thousand sounds,
words and music,
threats and songs of love,

pass through you each instant?
How marvelous it would be
if everything you carried
were at the service
of peace and goodness.

Do you feel the difference
between the flight of a bird
and the throb of an aircraft?
Do you see the spaceships
shooting by?
Do you go with them?
In those far reaches
is there still need of you?

No doubt you have knowledge
you cannot reveal.
No doubt you know well
the things beyond earth,
and always and everywhere
you feel in a wonderful way
the presence of your
Creator and Father.

Do you know that
you give us
of all images
one most close to God?

We live
inside God
everywhere
at all times,
just as we live
inside you.

And just as we
think rarely of you
by day and still

less at night,
so do we rarely
think of our God.

If we are without you
even a few seconds,
Life is unbearable!
Only then do we think
of you.
Our God fades from our thought
even more, yet he never
complains of the way
we leave him alone;
and he never leaves us!
O Air, please teach us
to think of you
and still more, much more,
to think of the Father,
our Creator and yours.

                                    —*SE*, 97–101

TREES, SISTER TREES

Ah, trees,
do you live in peace,
in harmony,
despite the differences
between you
which to the human eye
seem so immense?
How do you feel,
you towering palms,
you massive oaks,
you giant baobabs,
as you stare down upon
a tiny bush?

Are the fruit bearers,
apple, mango, and coconut,
tempted to mock
those who have simply
leaves and thorns?

Do you welcome
the birds' nests
and children who swing
from your branches?
What is it like
when the leaves fall
and your branches are draped
in snow?
Does spring give a hint
of the thought of resurrection?
And what is it like when
drought wounds the land
and you trees seem to raise
up your arms
in silent prayer
to our Lord and Father?

What do you feel
at the plucking of your fruits?
Is the stoning
the worst part?
And what is your pain
when your branches are pruned,
or when a tree entire
goes to the lumber yard
to be cut
into house or bridges or chairs or beds?
Do you understand the purpose
of a bridge
and the vivid symbol it is?
Do you realize your importance in
the building of a home?

Chairs and beds
call to mind rest
and make us think
of the family:
But what does it mean to you?

When lightning strikes a tree,
is it true that the tree
prefers itself to be struck
than to see a person or house
destroyed?

Remember, sister Tree,
that the Son of God
in order to reconcile us
with our Father and his,
bore a heavy cross.
Three times he fell
under that burden,
and wanted to die
nailed to the cross
in order to save us.

—SE, 103–5

MASS FOR THE CENTURY

O Century, our vehicle through time! This Mass is being celebrated expressly for you.

But first of all let us have the courage to ask ourselves the question: what is a century worth by God's standards? What is a century worth in relation to the progress of humanity?

By God's standards — forgive us, Century — a hundred years is no more than a drop in the ocean. When scholars investigate the age of the universe they lose themselves in millions and millions of years. It is frightening even to think in terms of light-years.

In relation to the progress of humanity, with the wild acceleration of history, ten years in modern times are the equivalent of fifty in the past, and twenty years almost call for centenary celebrations.

I shall not forget, O Century my friend, that I was almost present at your birth; and with a little effort I shall accompany you to the start of the next millennium....

But in any case I am one with Christ, one with him, as I begin this Eucharist, this thanksgiving in your name.

Do you know what I thank the Creator and Father for most of all? I thank him for uniting me, in Christ, with all human beings of every race, every color and creed.

Christ teaches us more and more that all of us, absolutely all of us, without exception, have the same Father; and that, consequently, we are all brothers! And further, we human beings sense that our fraternity extends to include all creatures, animated or inert, great or small. All of us emerged from the hands of the Creator!

Lending our voices joyfully to the stones and the seas, to the winds and the stars, to the trees and the animals, we are aware that above all we are brothers to our fellow men, sharing adventures and dangers, misery and glory....

O Century, our vehicle through time! Is it an exaggeration to say that today more than ever man is participating in the creative power of the Father in mastering nature and completing the work of creation? Kindling fire and inventing the wheel were among the first results of this participation. But today electronic computers are multiplying at an astonishing rate, and discoveries like nuclear energy and the boldness of journeys into space almost seem like an unwarranted invasion of God's own territory. But no! Our Father is incapable of jealousy! The more we advance, the more we attempt, the more we glorify the Creator and Father!

But it is a pity, O Century our friend, that while we are capable of both banishing misery from the earth and destroying all life in the universe, we continue to play this stupid game of manufacturing armaments that we know are powerful enough to mean suicide for all mankind.

It is a pity, O Century our friend, that as we begin to reach out toward the stars we leave behind us on earth an absurdity, a folly, an aberration: more than two-thirds of humanity living in subhuman conditions, suffering from poverty and starvation.

But what a joy it is, O Century, to see that God really isn't selfish. How the Creator and Father rejoices to make man his co-creator, how the Son of God, the redeemer of man and the universe, rejoices to make us his co-liberators!

Christ, the Son of God made man, who made himself our brother, urges us today more than ever to liberate ourselves and liberate our brothers and sisters from sin and the consequences of sin, from selfishness and the consequences of selfishness.

It is a pity, O Century, that as we continue to extend the limits of our intelligence and creativity we continue to be so limited, so grossly selfish and so incapable of imagining a world without empires to control and subjugate it. Incapable of imagining a world without oppressors and oppressed.

Nevertheless, O Century, in every country, and every race, and every religion, in every human group, the Spirit of God continues to inspire minorities who are resolved to make any sacrifice in order to create a world that is better to live in, more just and more humane: in order to liberate the world from the increasingly heavy and stifling structures that oppress practically all people.

What a joy it is to know that, without recourse to armed violence, young people — who have most reason for living! — will discover the secret of union between regions, between countries, between continents, between worlds. And then, animated by a love that is more powerful than death, we shall conquer war! We shall abolish racism! We shall suppress empires!

In centuries to come, human weakness will devise other oppressive structures. Selfishness will re-establish its ascendancy. Among the oppressed, underdogs, downtrodden, you will find many divisions, suspicions, cracks, and conflicts.

But rejoice, O Century our friend: we shall do the possible and the impossible to ensure that you pass on to the twenty-first century the victorious flame of a world without oppressors or oppressed, a world of brothers!

Onward, Century! Don't be an outsider at our Eucharist. Take an active part in our thanksgiving. Without hypocrisy, without pretending to be the greatest or the best, resolve to make any sacrifice in order to reach the threshold of the year two thousand deserving the title "the century of liberation"!

Do you know what I am asking of you now? That you awaken hopes, that you mobilize youth, and that you fight for the cause of unity.

You will find many people's hopes are faded, intermittent, or languishing. Many people are skeptical — or in despair. . . .

To those who are fortunate enough to believe in God the Creator and Father, you will point out that God did not create the world in order to amuse himself at our expense. He created the world and man out of love. Hatred will not have the last word.

To those who don't believe in God but have faith in man, you will point out that there is no point in half a faith. The only effective faith is total faith. True faith radiates hope and love.

If you meet young people of sixteen or eighteen or twenty who claim that life is absurd and question you about the meaning of their lives, make them understand that losing the joy of living is a sign of precocious old age. Make everyone understand, men and women of all ages, that we have a thousand reasons for living. They are wrong to think they have arrived too late in a world that is too old, where everything is already settled and there is nothing more to do!

Among the oppressed you will find a profusion of divisions, splits, distrust, and conflict. . . . Oppressors are skillful at sowing discord among the oppressed. It was no coincidence that at the supreme moment of his life Christ asked his Father for unity among his people. Suggest, teach, persuade: the day will come when all the world's minorities will unite to construct a world that is more just and more humane, the day when we shall finally discover the nuclear force of Love! — *CB*, 219–22

MODERN SPIRITUAL MASTERS
Robert Ellsberg, Series Editor

Already published:

Dietrich Bonhoeffer (edited by Robert Coles)
Simone Weil (edited by Eric O. Springsted)
Henri Nouwen (edited by Robert A. Jonas)
Pierre Teilhard de Chardin (edited by Ursula King)
Anthony de Mello (edited by William Dych, S.J.)
Charles de Foucauld (edited by Robert Ellsberg)
Oscar Romero (by Marie Dennis, Rennie Golden,
 and Scott Wright)
Eberhard Arnold (edited by Johann Christoph Arnold)
Thomas Merton (edited by Christine M. Bochen)
Thich Nhat Hanh (edited by Robert Ellsberg)
Rufus Jones (edited by Kerry Walters)
Mother Teresa (edited by Jean Maalouf)
Edith Stein (edited by John Sullivan, O.C.D.)
John Main (edited by Laurence Freeman)
Mohandas Gandhi (edited by John Dear)
Mother Maria Skobtsova (introduction by Jim Forest)
Evelyn Underhill (edited by Emilie Griffin)
St. Thérèse of Lisieux (edited by Mary Frohlich)
Flannery O'Connor (edited by Robert Ellsberg)
Clarence Jordan (edited by Joyce Hollyday)
G. K. Chesterton (edited by William Griffin)
Alfred Delp, S.J. (introduction by Thomas Merton)
Bede Griffiths (edited by Thomas Matus)
Karl Rahner (edited by Philip Endean)
Sadhu Sundar Singh (edited by Charles E. Moore)
Pedro Arrupe (edited by Kevin F. Burke, S.J.)